W9-COG-656

JUMPSTART
YOUR SERVICE
REVOLUTION

Transform Your Company's DNA
and Thrive in an Age of Disruption

Thomas Schlick

JUMPSTART YOUR SERVICE REVOLUTION:
TRANSFORM YOUR COMPANY'S DNA
AND THRIVE IN AN AGE OF DISRUPTION

ISBN: 978-0-9981779-1-5

Printed in the United States of America

Designed by Ivan Stojic

First Printing: 2018

www.ArtisanDigital.org
(651) 600-0178

Praise for Jumpstart Your Service Revolution

"*Jumpstart Your Service Revolution* provides a recipe for transforming your company into one that will thrive in a world rife with disruption. Digital transformation requires fundamental changes in technology as well as business models. Tom provides real-world lessons in service leadership in an easy-to-understand and simple-to-implement format. If you want your company to succeed in a world being quickly rewired for service, then listen to what Tom has to say!"

Bill Steenburgh
Senior Vice President, Pitney Bowes Global Services

"Harvard Business School Professor Clayton Christensen may have written the seminal book on disruption, but Tom's book explains *what a company can actually do* to battle such competitive disruption—and thrive!"

Gary Cohen
Founder and Managing Partner, CO2 Partners
Author of *Just Ask Leadership*

"Service is **the** competitive advantage in the twenty-first century digital world. Drawing on decades of experience leading service organizations at some of the world's most successful brands, Tom has created a step-by-step approach to transforming any organization into a service juggernaut. *If you want to jump to the head of the class in your industry, read Jumpstart Your Service Revolution!*"

John Carroll
CEO, The Service Council

"*Jumpstart Your Service Revolution* provides business leaders a compelling argument for organizational change. The challenge Tom outlines, grounded in historical examples, is a dire prognosis for long-term market success—UNLESS leadership makes an unbending commitment to systemic change throughout the organization. This book offers no quick, simple, "magic wand" delusions—rather it proposes a practical seven-point process, with proven results, to guide leadership to success."

Mike Gustafson
(Former) Worldwide President,
Sterilmed, Inc. (a Johnson & Johnson Company)

"*Jumpstart Your Service Revolution* is one of those very rare works that will stir you, challenging how you see your role and the way you do things. It's an astute look at how you can mold the future in your organization. Tom provides a powerful road map for anyone who wants to be a leader in our fast-changing world. And it's a fun read. If you're like me, you'll read this book more than once!"

Dean McPhee
CFO I Group Company Secretary,
Daniels International & Daniels Investments

"Tom's visionary management style is matched only by his ability to get your attention when he has a message that should be heard. In his new book, *Jumpstart Your Service Revolution*, Tom informs the reader that *'Ninety percent of the Fortune 500 companies that existed in 1955 have vanished...and 40% of the companies in the Fortune 500 today will be gone within ten years.'* He certainly has my attention! He then outlines a seven-point process for transformational change that will enable an organization to change not only its service delivery but its inherent DNA. I highly recommend this book to senior management as they build their strategy for survival and growth in an age of disruption."

Walt Gasparovic
Chairman & CEO, Society for Service Executives

"Finally, the message is driven home: Companies must not just *be aware* but must begin to *transform **now*** to be ready for the customer, cultural, and product shifts already affecting most industries. Tom's insight into recognizing the signals and making the right preparations is what our leaders need if they are to survive and prevail."

Jean Mork Bredeson
President, SERVICE 800

"In this amazing new book, Tom highlights how critical it is to transform how we work inside companies, and how the "employee experience" is just as crucial as the "customer experience." Organizations need to excel at both if they are to thrive in the next decade. Tom's book demonstrates how important it is to do just that, and what steps you need to take to get there!"

Lou Carbone
Founder & CEO, Experience Engineering

"Tom is a transformational leader with the ability to navigate disruptive change and achieve significant results. He knows how to build and sustain high-performing work teams that serve both external and internal customers. The seven-step process outlined in this book is a practical guide that will benefit any company facing disruptive change in their industry."

Tamara Tasche, MS., L.P.
VP of Executive and Transition Services, CPI Twin Cities

"Tom understands what it takes to change how companies do their work in an age of constant industry disruption. In *Jumpstart Your Service Revolution* he offers a seven-point process to achieve transformational change that is at the forefront of how today's leaders need to think and act!"

Clare Cizek
Partner, DHR International

"This succinct and easy-to-read book provides a well-defined, research and experience-based roadmap to transform any organization. All current and future leaders will benefit from reading, absorbing, and implementing Tom's recommendations."

James "Alex" Alexander
Founder, Alexander Consulting
Author of *Seriously Selling Services*

"I've seen Tom impact organizations as a senior executive for many years. So, it's a rare treat to have his collected wisdom at our fingertips. This book feels like you're sitting down with a senior executive who has done it before and having a conversation about both successes and failures, as he reveals his secret recipe for success. Packed with examples and take-aways, it's a delight to read. And it's essential for anyone who wants a solid foundation from which to lead in our transforming world."

Bruce Starcher
Managing Director, The Starcher Group

Preface

Do you sometimes feel that you are living your life, not just in the "fast lane," but in the "acceleration lane"? More change. More chaos. Less time. Less control. And woven in and around this feeling is the reality that your company—and your job—will be dramatically impacted by the disruptive forces marching toward your industry.

And you're trying your best to figure out what it all means—to skillfully navigate around the land mines hidden in the road ahead. You feel anxious, even somewhat fearful, about the relentless pace of change and the ever-increasing demands on your time and talent.

You look to your boss and the leaders within your company for clarity. While you hear their words, the actual responses seem a bit hollow. You have questions and concerns. Why are so many people on edge? Why am I feeling so much anxiety about the future? Why does it seem like our leaders are living in an alternate universe, talking about things that don't seem to really address the underlying issues? You begin to feel like you're living in a nightmare.

This is what it feels like when you are working in a company that is experiencing—or about to experience—significant industry disruption. And while all of this is distinctly unsettling on so many fronts, there also exists a bold opportunity to seize control of your situation and turn that nightmare into a vividly positive dream for the future.

You realize "change" is a must. And better yet, so do your company's leaders—the people that set the tone in an organization and model the culture within which everyone operates.

With that realization, the previous organizational headwinds now become tailwinds. You find yourself back in that "acceleration lane," but now it feels right and you begin to see the destination that lies ahead.

Turning those headwinds into tailwinds—and helping the corporation and the people that work in it see that future destination—is really what this book is all about. But it goes even further.

I have laid out a seven-step process that will guide you to this future destination, complete with road signs along the way. These road signs will give you a relative sense of where you are along the journey as well as warning you when a sharp curve lies ahead.

The good news is you can confront disruptive change head-on and come out a winner, not simply a bystander reading your company's obituary.

You have a golden opportunity to transform your company's DNA and be part of the future vs. the corporate road-kill you see on the side of the road as you look in your rear-view mirror.

I hope this book helps you ask the right questions and understand when the winds of change arrive, and inspires you and your company's leaders to do what it takes to thrive in an age of disruption.

Tom Schlick

Table of Contents

PART ONE
PRIORITIES

CHAPTER ONE

CHAPTER TWO

CHAPTER THREE

PART TWO
PRACTICES

Part One
PRIORITIES

Extinction Is Real

"The greatest danger for most of us isn't that our aim is too high and we miss it, but that our aim is too low and we reach it."

Michelangelo

Imagine yourself in a situation where nothing is going well. You mentally thrash about, searching for a solution. Something is missing, but you can't put your finger on it.

That's a common personal experience. You eventually settle on an answer and embark on resolving your dilemma—only to discover your solution was just temporary or maybe downright wrong—and you're plunged back into that foggy unsureness.

Now imagine this same state of foggy unsureness in your job. The CEO is explaining the company's mission statement, and you haven't the slightest idea what the words really mean. All you remember is "shareholder value."

I don't know anybody who goes to bed at night dreaming of maximizing shareholder value. Well, I take that back. I know a few, but I'm not sure what the sky color is in their world.

Or how about when senior leaders roll out annual goals and objectives, and you count a dozen "number one priorities." It isn't actually presented that way. But it's clear that each must be accomplished first and fast!

Then there are the monthly town halls, gatherings of everyone who can fit in a room or join a conference call. You're lucky if they happen monthly, because companies seem to have moved to even less frequent gatherings, which is crazy when you're trying to keep your teams informed and up to date. You sit alongside your team, listening as senior management answers tough questions from the crowd. The senior leaders answer in code, with words that don't seem to match the numbers you see onscreen.

As a senior leader, I've been on the delivering end of this, and I'm not proud of my muddled communication. When the news isn't good, leaders want to be clear without creating panic or disillusionment, but you know you've lost the audience when their eyes glaze over and the fog rolls in.

I'll say right now that I learned from that experience and now work hard to give clear, precise answers.

And what happens after the town hall? Have you watched the body language as everyone leaves the room? Any good news doesn't stick for long, and bad news creates lingering fear and mistrust, a gnawing feeling that something is missing. You hear whispering in hallways or breakrooms or across cubicles. Teammates ask uncomfortable questions. "Why isn't our strategy clear?" "They say sales are off, but they never get at root causes. They just say next month will be better." "New products are late again. Why can't R&D get things done?"

That begs an even deeper question. "Why are the functions R&D depends on not working with the same urgency to get new products through Engineering and Quality and into production?"

Sometimes questions get more personal and disconcerting. "What will happen if we miss our targets? Will people be laid off? Should I be looking for another job?"

Soon the real question becomes obvious, like a cancer eating away at confidence in the organization. "Why isn't senior leadership doing anything to make our situation better?" "All they do is lock themselves up in all-day meetings. Why don't they ask what WE think?" "What in the world are they DOING?"

You assume they're reviewing their plentiful goals and objectives.

I've seen those agendas, one PowerPoint presentation after another, all day long. As the hours tick by, senior leaders who are virtual slip away to the airport to fly home without ever stepping out to engage the larger employee group.

Because leaders spend all their time in conference rooms, the average employee couldn't match the names and faces of specific senior leaders, even if the leaders were put in a line-up and the employee given a hint. Most of the senior leaders are unknown and unrelatable. This lack of a relationship with everyday employees can't be good.

Nothing that senior management discusses or decides gets shared with middle management or the larger team. The bits that leak are masked in code and filtered, so others read into them whatever they want. Employees are left confused and frustrated, and their trust in their boss and senior leadership continues to erode.

Sometime later, the next all-day senior leader staff meeting occurs. Nothing real is disseminated beyond that room. Employees get another quarterly town hall with more of the same. The merry-go-round comes full circle.

What happens next? People hunker down to do their jobs but nothing extra. Across the organization, communication and cross-functional collaboration weaken. Ironically, senior leaders are hidden away for another all-day meeting, discussing this year's employee engagement survey and high-fiving each other for all the good things they're doing to boost morale. But not a single senior leader ever ventures out of the conference room to simply listen to what the everyday people have to say. Leaders never hear about employee concerns, or better yet, about their personal goals and how the company can help.

If you could step outside the situation and gain a big-picture perspective, you would see a company adrift. Honest communication goes missing. Morale suffers. Trust plummets. Careers stall. Good employees leave. Customer loyalty wanes as the company falters on meeting commitments. Financial results are mixed, and in the worst-case scenario, the company heads into a slow death spiral.

The organization might not die. But senior management turns over. New leadership arrives with new strategies. Optimism grows. Then the long-standing company culture seeps back in and blurs communication and focus. Things that were supposed to get better, don't. Oh, some battles are won, and leadership says that more winning lies ahead. But those are just words, and the circle of frustration and missed opportunities continues until the next big change occurs.

The Dying and Dead

Most people have seen and experienced this at some point in their work-life. Picture for a moment what must have been going on in hundreds or thousands of companies over the years that saw themselves in that slow death spiral, heading for extinction. I doubt it was a newsflash for most people that something was horribly wrong. They knew it, but nothing was done. Maybe nothing could be done. Yet most had that gnawing feeling that something was missing. But what?

Why does this phenomenon keep recurring? From what I've seen, companies in this situation all have:

- Smart, experienced senior leaders

- Employees with long tenures and institutional knowledge

- People with the right education

- Strategies for the future with annual goals and objectives

- Proven successes

- Town halls or group meetings to communicate with employees

- Products or services that customers want

- Employees who saw the iceberg ahead but were not collectively able to steer the company to safety

In addition, senior leaders had countless constructive resources they could tap—McKinsey & Company, Accenture, Deloitte, and PWC to name a few. These companies thrive on advising organizations on corporate strategy, technology direction, new product pipeline, markets to serve, optimal organizational structure, and detailed competitor analysis.

We could also layer on all the business authors who have provided tremendous insights on moving from good to great or achieving a differentiable and sustainable strategic advantage. And how to get the right people on the bus and create a winning culture.

Despite all this horsepower, countless companies couldn't get out of their own way and found themselves headed for extinction. People within the company saw it coming but were helpless to change things.

Here's just a short list of companies that have gone bust, were swallowed by another company, or still struggle today (see Table 1). This list represents a handful of the hundreds of examples I could list from online searches and studying businesses throughout my career.

This list touches just a few well-known brands. What is the common denominator? At first glance, there isn't one. Companies that are dying and dead display these characteristics:

- All industry sectors

- High-tech and low-tech products

- Companies large and small

- Public and privately held

- Service businesses

- Serve global and U.S.-only markets

- Strong, charismatic leaders and those that don't want the spotlight

- Experienced great past success

- Very competent middle-management teams

- Historically good customer loyalty

TABLE 1: Companies that have gone out of business or been acquired, or are currently in deep trouble

A&P Grocery Stores	Levitz Furniture
Amoco Oil	Linens & Things
Bethlehem Steel	Macy's
Blockbuster Video	Northwest Airlines
Border Books	Pan Am
Circuit City	Pets.com
Eastern Airlines	RadioShack
EF Hutton	Sears/Kmart
GameStop	Sports Authority
hhgregg	Washington Mutual
Kodak	Westinghouse
Lehman Brothers	Woolworths

What's the takeaway? Failure is agnostic. Something deeper is going on that is pervasive across these companies. And the facts back this up.

Ninety percent of the Fortune 500 companies that existed in 1955 have vanished. And since the year 2000, 50% of the Fortune 500 companies have disappeared! Some of those organizations went bankrupt and died. Others merged or were acquired. Is that so bad? Probably! Even in the best of circumstances, those endings represent the extinction of a company with accomplishments and ideals once celebrated. And it certainly meant lost opportunities, especially for the many employed at these companies. Dreams unfulfilled, careers stalled, families in turmoil, and everyone left asking WHY? HOW DID THIS HAPPEN?

The future doesn't look any brighter. Many experts forecast that 40% of the companies in the Fortune 500 today will be gone within ten years![1]

That's staggering. But not surprising.

Shouldn't we expect change? Isn't this just the life-cycle of companies? Perhaps the life-and-death or success-and-failure cycle of an individual company doesn't matter. But maybe you'll see it matters when you are life-cycled out of a job. Or your community loses a major employer. Or yet another local business is now directed by a far-off parent company that lacks true existential concern for your corner of the world.

And why do organizations come and go?

---

1   John M. Olin School of Business at Washington University.

Poor strategies, multiplied by poor execution, compounded by poor management. Robert Kaplan, creator of the Balanced Scorecard, says the overwhelming cause of strategic planning failure is poor execution. And Kotter International determined that, on average, 70% of new, large-scale strategic initiatives fall short of their goal, as did a similar McKinsey & Company study.

Sobering stories. Painful statistics. All point to one fact. Every company today faces a dire ultimatum: change or die.

Disruptors and Disruption

Of course, organizations don't live and die unto themselves. They vie for survival amid threats old and new. The disruptors of modern business are well documented, including digital transformation, massive globalization, e-commerce, virtual management structures, a diverse workforce, diminishing employee loyalty, and customers who demand more and more—coupled with their viral threats of bolting to the competition.

The months and years ahead will bring even more rapid disruption. Digital technologies, Robotic Process Automation (RPA), Cognitive Automation (CA), Internet of Things (IoT), and Big Data/Analytics are just a few technologies that will create significant turmoil for existing market-leading companies.

Organizations that are less tech-savvy or welcoming of diversity are likely losers, and shifting demographics loom as an issue all its own. The throngs of baby boomers leaving the workforce take extensive institutional knowledge with them as they exit, although millennials moving into leadership positions will gain elbow room to make their mark.

Customers will increasingly expect outcome-based solutions vs. discrete products and services. "Outcomes" include choosing Uber over car ownership, for example, especially if costs come down because of driverless vehicles. Or instead of buying tires for your car, you might purchase "miles of tire usage."

Seem far-fetched? Don't kid yourself. Disruptive change will be everywhere. (By the way, Uber's market capitalization is equal to that of General Motors, and Google is filing for more patents around self-driving cars than any of the mainstream automotive companies.)

These rapid changes collide with age-old pressures of fighting off new competitors, reducing costs, and retaining talented employees.

As industries transform, most companies fail to learn and adapt. Specifically, market leaders fall prey to the "Innovator's Dilemma" described by Clayton Christenson. Many top companies do most everything right and still fall prey to disruptive competitors. Leaders see the threat! But their efforts remain focused on the tried-and-true, like targeting existing customers, pursuing ever-higher profits, and doubling down on whatever made them successful in the first place. These companies play the game by the existing rules while disruptive companies innovate by changing the rules!

Companies that fail to learn and adapt are companies that die. Senior leaders may see the disruption coming yet continue their present trajectory. Companies are doomed when they relentlessly pursue their current business model without addressing their need to compete within a new set of rules.

Something is missing.

Your World

How are technological and market changes disrupting your industry—and your specific organization? Are your company's senior leaders making things happen—or letting things happen to them? Does that uneasy feeling in your gut tell you things are heading in the wrong direction—despite what senior management says? Who in your company sees the need for change—and who is listening?

You might be facing down what used to be called a "Kodak Moment." That term once meant an opportunity to get a great picture. Now I believe it exemplifies failure to change, as when Kodak clung to its film business, completely missing a digital future.

So where do we go from here? What can we do for companies failing to deal with disruption? Can we alter the trajectory toward extinction that seems present in virtually every company's DNA? Can we learn to thrive amid disruption? This book provides answers.

I've spent my career in senior executive roles with companies large and small, public and private. These organizations represent a wide cross-section of industries, including aerospace, industrial automation, financial services, secure ID, transportation, office products and solutions, healthcare, and medical devices. With this background, I offer first-hand expertise gained by leading from the inside, both succeeding and failing. To these personal examples, I will add research, case studies, and the thoughtful insights of others.

While every company is markedly different, they all share the same fundamental flaw that causes companies to fail and die.

As you can discern from the title of this book, the road to future success isn't paved with evolutionary thinking. Rather, the necessary changes are highly transformational. They happen at the innermost core of a company, the DNA that makes an organization what it is.

Small change wearies most people. Big change—transformational change—maxes out most employees' resistance meter! But here's my discovery. Transformational change is especially difficult because the process rarely starts until a company is already in trouble. It may have taken years to get to this point, and now the company and its employees stand at a crossroads. Which way to turn?

My experience shows that more often than not, senior leaders make the wrong turn. Their past success predisposes them to make decisions in the same old way. Senior leaders don't see storm clouds brewing—and so make wrong choices when the storm hits—because of a handful of critical dysfunctional behaviors most senior leaders exhibit.

This habit of doing the same old, same old is the root of the problem.

In the coming chapters, I will identify these critical dysfunctional behaviors and offer specific tactics and actions to address them.

Even more importantly, I will then offer steps to address these behaviors within the context of leading transformational change throughout the organization, by showing what transformational change looks like and how you can achieve it. This process need not be a mystery made cumbersome by fancy words.

The path forward is to JUMPSTART THE SERVICE REVOLU-
TION within your company!

Read on to understand what this means, why it's so critical,
and the steps you can take to make it happen.

CHAPTER ONE TAKEAWAYS

- Any change is difficult. *Transformational change* is even more difficult.

- History demonstrates that many companies can't—and don't—make the changes needed. They stagnate, get acquired, or disappear altogether.

- The irony in most companies is that a few smart people see the disruptive change coming, but they are powerless to alter the company's direction.

- Failure is agnostic. Companies that don't change come from all industry sectors. They can be large or small, public or private.

- The digital transformation disrupting many industries will only accelerate the problem and create an even more urgent need to adopt a successful transformational change initiative.

- A handful of critical dysfunctional behaviors by senior leaders are at the root of the problem.

- The path to success is to jumpstart the Service Revolution in your company.

CHAPTER TWO

Transform Your Company's DNA

"At first people refuse to believe
that a strange new thing can be done,
then they begin to hope that it can be done,
then they see that it can be done,
then it's done and all the world wonders
why it wasn't done centuries ago."

FRANCES BURNETT

D isruption is real. Its pace is accelerating. If you're not already experiencing major upheaval, it's coming soon to an industry near you.

Of course, there are shining examples of companies reinventing themselves. Amazon, for instance, has banned the use of PowerPoint when presenting issues and updates to management. A small change, but its symbolic impact is huge. Speak up! Say what needs to be said! Don't bury tough truths in a slide deck!

Amazon, a disruptor now three decades old, needs continual transformation. So does an American stalwart born 102 years earlier.

General Electric once promoted itself with ads of giant steam turbines or appliances. Today it showcases predictive maintenance of jet engines using digital technology. The appliance group has been sold off, cast into the trash bin of company history.

GE is so serious about its transformation that it recently swapped out its key leader. CEO Jeffrey Immelt—leader for more than 15 years—gave way to Joe Flannery, a veteran of GE's healthcare business. Flannery promises to reexamine everything. Nothing is off the table.[2]

GE is also relocating its corporate headquarters from Stamford, Connecticut to Boston, Massachusetts, home to a large, vibrant high-tech educational community headlined by Harvard, MIT, and Northeastern. In fact, more than half a million undergrads and graduate students make the city fully one-quarter millennial, third highest in the nation, just behind Madison, Wisconsin and Pittsburgh, Pennsylvania.[3]

Oh, and one more thing. GE has ditched the annual employee performance review. More on that later.

Amazon and GE and a handful of other existing companies are the exceptions, addressing disruption by proactively transforming themselves from the inside out.

---

2   *Wall Street Journal*, June 13, 2017.

3   *Wall Street Journal*, May 17, 2017.

Seeing the Future

One only needs to look at the disruption caused by the likes of Netflix, Airbnb, or Uber to see how breakthrough innovations change entire industries, along with the fortunes of those who fail to keep up.

In most companies, someone sees the disruption coming. Ironically, this significant observation typically occurs lower in the organization and NOT among senior leadership. Those who see the impending clash with a new reality implore management to "Do something!" Frequently, they're not just ignored but scorned. Insightful workers keep quiet, preferring not to be labeled a heretic (or to risk their all-important performance review rating and associated pay bump).

When companies fail to respond to industry disruptions, they lose revenues and profits. People lose their jobs, and a new industry order arises.

Why do we accept this as an inevitability? If senior management had more foresight, if only they had listened to the crazy predictions of a lower-level employee, then maybe things would have turned out differently. But more often than not, they don't listen, and the rest is history.

Here's a real-world example.

I assumed responsibility for a quick-ship distribution business. I embraced the role, which I saw as a learning opportunity that meshed well with my other responsibilities.

My style is to go to the frontlines, where I can observe the work and ask questions. And as I met with supervisors of various regional distribution centers, I was startled by what I learned.

The supervisors seemed capable, customer-oriented, and energized by the new leadership change. I asked these leaders to identify key performance metrics and report how their locations were faring. I learned that their quick-ship goal was two weeks. Yes. Two weeks. The average distribution center met that lofty goal 65% of the time. And for this exceptional service, our customers paid a 10% premium.

My instinctive thought—not knowing anything—was that a commitment to get product out the door in two weeks didn't sound like quick-ship. Missing the mark a third of the time couldn't be good. When the distribution supervisors tried to convince me this was maximum performance, I wasn't sure whether to cringe or cry or both.

I felt the business would grow faster if we performed to that 10% price premium. Right or wrong, I declared we needed a new definition of quick.

My common-sense metric was to get product out the door no more than two or three days after receipt of order. Preferably the same day. And it should happen with a 98% on-time performance. The distribution supervisors declared this virtually impossible. Asked why, they pointed to existing process.

At the time, the only available process tools were Total Quality Management (TQM) and W. Edwards Deming's 14 Points. No lean Six Sigma. No value-mapping. Common sense told me we should start with a single distribution center and document every process step from customer order to completed shipment.

By the time we finished recording every step of our shipping process, the hard-copy documentation ran six-and-a-half feet end-to-end. With copious details in hand, we challenged each step. Why was it done? Was it essential? How could we make it faster? My goal was an honest, real-world solution, meaning that if a process step was necessary, we kept it. Changing our workflow and layout was fair game, but I wouldn't set the team up for failure by omitting essentials. I knew I might be proven wrong about raising performance metrics, but I trusted the data would take us in the right direction.

At one point, I asked why we manually duplicated each order in a paper logbook. The supervisors' answer was classic. "We've always done it that way."

"Why?" I asked.

"That's how Mary did it. It's what she taught us."

"How do we use the log?"

Shrugs. No one knew. If the step once mattered, it now looked like a dead-end with no current value.

"How long has Mary been gone?"

"Three years."

For years we had diligently duplicated every order—manually. In a log no one used. We cut that step. We continued to eliminate steps or modify workflow until our process document shrank to under two feet. We repeated the evaluation at four more distribution centers.

Everyone felt energized around the change and was sure it would improve performance. We just didn't know how much.

Fast forward a year. The quick-ship business tripled. We averaged 98% on-time and delivered within two days. The distribution teams felt empowered to make changes and improvements. By eliminating meaningless work, everyone's "new" jobs felt like a major upgrade. And ecstatic customers gladly signed up for a 10% price premium.

In most companies, the processes we follow—the expectations of how we do our jobs—are passed down like tribal knowledge. When someone calls out an institutional blind spot, change is often impossible because "we've always done it that way."

External Service Satisfaction

No modern company can survive offering "quick-ship" at a premium when essential product isn't headed out the door almost instantaneously. Common sense and our own consumer buying habits tell us that much. But my simple story exemplifies countless processes and departments in many organizations, across many industries. These institutional blind-spots are widespread across company, industry, and geography.

Companies today—particularly large companies—focus untold resources on satisfying and even delighting their customers, the people who pay for their products and services. These companies build large service organizations, with huge contact centers ready and able to answer customer requests. Their sophisticated cloud-based service-management systems capture data from dozens of customer touchpoints, then crunch the data to learn even more about how to satisfy the customer.

As a result, we prize Service Excellence, giving the customer exactly what they want in a way that catches them by surprise. The term "Service Excellence" was first used by Price Pritchett in a booklet with that title published in 1989, so this concept has had ample time to become entrenched practice. We identify "service champions" as individuals or whole companies that take ownership of the customer relationship in a way that reaches out proactively, accepts accountability, and exudes positivity, all to make the customer feel special.

Today there are Customer Satisfaction Surveys, Net Promotor Scores, Customer Experience and Customer Effort metrics, and Customer User Forums, as well as front-line sales and service people whose primary focus is to keep the customer happy. Moreover, a far-reaching industry of companies provides expertise to help organizations improve their customer service and overall customer experience. My recent Google search of "Customer Satisfaction and Customer Experience Companies" turned up 2.4 million hits. That's a lot of help!

The benefits of happy customers are amplified customer loyalty, increased revenues and profit, more repeat business, greater market share, more insight into future new product and service needs, higher shareholder value, and larger market capitalization for the company. To be specific, industry metrics show a 5% increase in customer loyalty can create a 95% increase in company profitability. Keep in mind that it can cost up to 23 times more to acquire a new customer than to retain one you already have.

As I said earlier, there is no downside to delivering external Service Excellence.

Internal Customer Service

So here is my fundamental question. I hope it becomes your burning issue: Why haven't companies translated this extensive knowledge and experience of EXTERNAL customer service into improving INTERNAL customer service?

Today, most writing and tools focus on front-line customer service. The rest of the organization gets a pass. Yet when every employee understands that "serving the customer" is the job of all, then they see themselves either serving customers directly or serving someone who does. The ultimate benefit is that a company focused on serving external AND internal customers is better poised to identify and aggressively react to transformational change within its industry.

Here's my contention: The solution to company-killing disruption is to create a service-centered, customer-centric culture throughout a company where ALL employees can become service champions. And this new way of working won't happen without a Service Revolution in the company. This is the only way I know to ignite transformational change within a company and ensure its chance at a thriving future.

You might be shaking your head, feeling like you've already got this dialed in. I politely and respectfully disagree, and I'll illustrate with another real-life example from a large company.

A few days into a new role at this organization, I discovered the documentation system was still entirely manual. I'm not talking about the distant past. This scene is recent history. Electronic documentation systems were everywhere.

Each project in this large company required a minimum of 50 or 60 documents be prepared, reviewed, and signed off. In this all-manual system, you can imagine how documents would get stranded on people's desks, and you couldn't begin to know where they were lost. If a document wasn't signed within a reasonable time, it was considered invalid, and the arduous journey started again. Sometimes again—and again!

The average time to get a document signed was 35 days. People begged for an electronic document system. Cost wasn't the problem. It just didn't make the IT or company priority list.

Everyone was frustrated. Locating lost folders was a colossal waste of time. Remote employees actually needed the document emailed to them to sign, scan, and resend.

That was the best case. Imagine all the changes inserted by five departments MARKING UP THE DOCUMENT WITH A RED PEN. Changes had to be incorporated, and revised documents needed to be rerouted and re-signed.

This manual document system impacted all quality and compliance activities, all new product development activities, and all customer issues needing analysis.

Like most companies, this one had a mission statement etched into the wall about the high importance of serving employees, serving customers, and so on. Was that a cynically hollow promise—or just another blind spot?

I believe that thousands of similar examples exist in most companies. They're present in global giants and small organizations, startups and Fortune 500 behemoths. Everywhere there is consequential work done inefficiently, leading to frustrated employees, a detached-from-reality senior leadership, and worst of all, customers who don't get what they want when they want it, whether orders, shipments, invoices, issue resolution, or new products.

When customers leave, the offending company wonders why. They're in active denial. There's no introspection to understand the real reasons customers bolt. It must have been competitive price pressure, right?

All of this makes the journey to implement a service-centered, customer-concentric culture INSIDE the company for all INTERNAL people, functions, and departments so critical. Done right, studies have shown that:

- Employee Engagement goes up by 20%+

- Company costs not valued by the customer decrease by 20%+

- Customer satisfaction scores improve by 20%+

The Internal Customer's Perspective

It's time to think hard about the pervasive change that needs to occur to create a service-centered, customer-centric culture inside a company and throughout its many functions.

Just for a moment, put yourself in the shoes of an INTERNAL customer. Imagine yourself and every coworker from the top to the bottom of your organization as a customer of every other. Each person ultimately works for the good of the EXTERNAL customer. Now ask yourself, "Is the company easy to do business with?"

As I do that exercise, picturing various companies I have known as an employee, consultant, or another close observer, here's what I have concluded.

We're steeped in an assembly-line mentality. Each person and department dutifully does its part. However, we're all so focused on our individual roles that even our most urgent requests often get slow responses from others, because we're all head-down in our own tasks. Requests often meet push-back of "not my job," and it feels like we're being passed off from person to person.

Meanwhile, our coworkers who face external customers are tasked with being that "one touchpoint" the outside world loudly demands. But those external-facing coworkers rely on the rest of us to answer customer questions and resolve issues. Those of us with internal roles don't have customer service embedded in our work psyche, and that mindset and behaviors certainly aren't written in our annual performance goals.

As a result, the external customer often waits while internal mechanisms slowly crank out a response. The company is proud of itself for resolving the external customer's issue, yet the customer feels like a wet baby who was passed among relatives until someone finally takes care of her. And as all of this plays out, management assumes everything is fine.

Is that how we want the company to work?

What we want isn't an assembly line but an orchestra playing a beautiful symphony! All the musical instruments are
the functions and departments in the company. Importantly,
all the players read from one sheet of music. Internal and
external customers hear great music, all in harmony with
their expectations.

How is your company perceived? How do you experience it
internally? Is it an assembly line of departments, each working autonomously and independently, making noise and no
music? Or is it a well-tuned orchestra, with every instrument
playing off the same sheet of music in harmony with customer
expectations?

Imagine the latter becoming the culture of your company.
That vision is what you need to succeed in the world you face
today and into the future. The speed of business is accelerating,
disruptive change is impacting most industries and companies,
the barriers to entry in most business are constantly falling,
and expectations of excellence are continually rising. Your
customers who show patience today will switch in a heart-
beat tomorrow if you don't continually provide them with a
significantly better experience.

If you doubt this is true, go back and revisit the list of once-
mighty companies noted in chapter one. Companies can no
longer feel entitled to retain their current business. They must
go out and earn it every day.

Jumpstart the Service Revolution

If you're already doing a pretty good job on "Customer Satisfaction" with your current customers out on the front-lines, why wouldn't you take this opportunity to inject a service-centered, customer-centric culture to all people, functions, and departments within your company? Your employees will be more engaged. Costs not valued by the customer will fall away. And your company will stand a far better chance of surmounting the disruptive forces of change striking your industry.

Do you want to transform your company's DNA? Jumpstart your Service Revolution!

In the chapters ahead, we will dive into how to jumpstart the Service Revolution in your company. We'll expose the critical behaviors your senior leaders need to change to incubate and grow the Service Revolution. Then we'll examine how new behaviors become the part of how your company operates every day. These fresh habits will have a significant positive impact on culture, employee engagement, employee turnover, cross-functional collaboration—and end customer success!

There is no downside to a successful Service Revolution!

CHAPTER TWO TAKEAWAYS

- To respond to disruption, we need to jumpstart the Service Revolution within the company.

- Our actions will ignite a transformational change within the organization that enables it to better see and address the disruptive changes occurring in many industries.

- Ignoring change virtually guarantees that your company's future won't be as bright as your past— and you may even cease to exist!

- We covered two real-life examples:

  - Distribution: Institutional blind spots are difficult to change because "we have always done it that way."

  - Electronic Documentation System: Well-funded companies that should know better often do not act to do the right thing for internal and external customers.

- Consider how your external AND internal customers must see you. Are you an assembly line or an orchestra?

CHAPTER THREE

Three Leadership Dysfunctions

"Vision without action is merely a dream. Action without vision just passes the time. Vision with action can change the world."

JOEL BARKER

W hy don't companies and senior leadership teams extend the same customer satisfaction mindset and behaviors they so ardently practice with EXTERNAL customers to their INTERNAL people, functions, and departments? Think of:

- Engineering

- R&D

- Marketing

- IT

- Finance

- HR

- Manufacturing

- Operations

- Supply Chain

- Quality and Compliance

- Regulatory

- Business Development

- Environmental Health and Safety

- Administration

- Legal

...and any other support function that exists inside of a company, in addition to the traditional customer service group, call center, field service, etc.

If a customer service mindset isn't flourishing throughout a company, don't blame the people doing those jobs. That isn't where the problem starts. The real issue is that senior leaders exhibit critical dysfunctional behaviors that suppress the rest of the company's responses to industry disruption.

I've identified the top three dysfunctional behaviors senior leaders must change for the Service Revolution to occur. Left unchallenged, they're a potent cocktail for preserving the status quo:

- Saying one thing and doing another

- Care you show vs. show you care

- When everything is a priority, nothing is a priority

Companies die because they have developed rust within their culture through many years of experiencing specific dysfunctional behaviors by their senior leaders. These dysfunctions create accepted norms and employee attitudes NOT in sync with a culture of true Service Excellence. This misalignment negatively impacts ALL the external and internal service transactions that occur every day—all day, all week, all year, all the time.

The easiest way to grasp this is to examine a few real-life examples showing how even companies proud of their exceptional service to end customers fail within their organizations. These breakdowns expose the soft underbelly of a dysfunctional organization, underscoring the necessity of the Service Revolution even in companies that assume they're already on the journey. We'll see specific situations for which these companies were unprepared, despite their status as Service Champions in the marketplace.

A Simple Example

Picture a design engineer whose job description focuses solely on new product development. Her goals for the year dictate that she develop a specified number of widgets. Nothing in her goals requires getting them through production and launched into the marketplace. Just development, pure and simple.

When one of this engineer's new products hangs up in manufacturing, Operations wants her help addressing the issue. The engineer could deliver a rapid fix, but she reminds herself that Operations has a smart team of manufacturing engineers. Finding a solution will be a good learning experience. So the design engineer excuses herself from any further responsibility.

To the engineer, helping Operations is a big time-waste that could mess with her development schedule, not to mention her performance rating and future compensation. Of course, Operations feels irritated, and cross-functional collaboration takes a hit. Worse yet, it takes Operations another six months to get the product out, costing the company $2 million in lost sales.

Was this engineer delivering a good internal service experience? Did she ever consider Operations was her customer?

I'm guessing the engineer saw her boss as the internal customer because the boss was counting how many new products the engineer could generate. You might assume that common sense would persuade the engineer to help the Operations team. They all work for the same company, right?

It didn't. Common sense wasn't enough to help this company launch new products faster.

Now think of all the departments or groups within a company where something similar goes badly wrong. Consider how many job descriptions, policies, procedures, performance metrics, work instructions, training courses, mission and company values statements, and cultural norms exist. What are the consequences of NOT following these formal and informal mandates, even if common sense says the employee should deviate from what's expected? Finally, mix in all the employees whose managers and leaders keep them hidden in silos, unavailable to the rest of the company (despite management's battle cry for better cross-functional collaboration).

Having done that thought exercise, it isn't hard to imagine where and how everyday problems compound within companies. For example:

- Could it be possible that an accounts receivable team might not be clear with the sales team that the company is writing off too much bad debt?

- Or when the Marketing Department determines the list prices for new products, how strongly do they listen to sales about what the customer would accept—or better, what the competition is doing?

- Or could it be that the Quality and Regulatory team focuses more on compliance to quality procedures, escalations, and CAPAs (Corrective Actions, Preventive Actions) than signing new product documents?

Think of the repercussions when employees lack an internal customer service mindset. I understand, for example, when people say, "quality is job number one." Common sense tells us no one wants poor quality. But when that becomes the Quality team's only mantra—and new product development and launch suffer—how does that help external customers? How does it help people downstream who are measured on new product launches? Or senior leaders' committed to achieving the company's top goals?

Pervasive Impact

I strongly believe the behaviors and actions I've briefly described are rampant and pervasive in most companies, even well-run companies! Why do I believe this? Because I've seen and experienced many of these behaviors in the companies I have worked with. As a prolific networker, I've heard hundreds of people share similar experiences within their organizations.

What I've seen and heard leads me to believe that the more prevalent the top three dysfunctional behaviors, the more pervasive the embedded problems. Said differently, practices we would never get away with in the marketplace—with external customers—are commonplace inside our companies. Over time, these practices sap a company's energy, with the ultimate outcome of extinction.

You can understand why these practices become so deeply embedded. Companies organize around a hierarchical structure ruled by policies, procedures, job descriptions, stated company goals, performance reviews, and cultural norms. Without these things, there would be anarchy and chaos.

Or so people say.

In part, they're right. Yet when these practices take on a life of their own and dominate how people interact—and how they are measured—and how they are compensated—then we have created what I call "institutional disservice."

When you bump up against instances of institutional disservice, then a new way of thinking about "work" and "customers" and "workplace behaviors" is essential. It isn't enough to assume people will heed common sense and do what is right, especially given how long it takes for people and cultures to change.

This gets at the heart of jumpstarting the Service Revolution.

Jumpstarting the Service Revolution means changing company culture, and I mean REALLY CHANGING it. No culture programs, no slogans, no short-term efforts, no feel-good initiatives, no one-and-done management meetings where the CEO claims things will be better in the future simply by declaring it so.

In fact, here's a good example of what the Service Revolution isn't.

Target Corporation has been in the news for their struggling financial performance. Profits have slipped considerably, and their grocery operation appears to be in chaos. Senior leaders have left the company, including Casey Carl, former Chief Innovation and Strategy Officer. Carl's job was spearheading innovation at Target.

Even as Carl pushed Target to consider the direction of retail beyond the next few years and implement innovations, the company was dismantling his leading-edge projects to focus on old fallbacks of remodeling stores and lowering prices.[4]

That doesn't seem very innovative, yet Target CEO Brian Cornell says, "Innovation is alive and well at Target. Our new leader's job will be to build upon the progress we've made. And while this leader will play a critical role in Target's innovation story, it's not the story they will write alone. Innovation must

---

4   *Minneapolis Star Tribune*, April 21, 2017.

be a mindset, an essential component of every business, every strategy, and every team."[5]

Wow! Nice words. But how do we reconcile them with the usual priorities of store remodeling and cutting prices? What will fundamentally change in Target's day-to-day operating policies, procedures, and performance metrics to reward employees for living into an innovation mindset?

Likely very little. Why? Because the Service Revolution hasn't started at Target. It might never begin if the focus remains on remodeling and price reductions.

Do I see Clayton Christenson's shadow lurking in Target's boardroom?

Changing company culture is difficult. Some would say almost impossible. It's been said that fewer than 20% of culture change initiatives within companies succeed.

Any culture change MUST start at the top of the organization, with the CEO minding the right things with the right metrics to even have a chance at succeeding. Most CEOs begin with good intentions but fail to follow through where and when it's most critical.

Before going deeper into jumpstarting the Service Revolution and the critical senior leadership behaviors that need to change, two more real-world examples will set the stage.

---

5   *Minneapolis Star Tribune*, April 21, 2017.

CASE STUDY:
The United Airlines Fiasco

By almost every measure, the airline industry has been rocking along. Airline revenues and profitability are up, costs are down, flight delays are down, lost luggage is down, and customer satisfaction scores are up.

So how does an airline with the moniker "Fly the Friendly Skies" end up dragging a paying customer off a plane, as other horrified passengers look on? Caught on cell phone video, the scene went viral. Pulled from his seat and dragged headfirst down the jet aisle, the passenger suffered broken facial bones and knocked-out teeth, all because United wanted to get four of its employees from O'Hare in Chicago to nearby Louisville so they could start a shift. If that wasn't enough, the United CEO smeared the customer, initially casting him as the problem and not the victim.

And what did United get out of this? A huge decline in their market capitalization, a CEO derailed from a promised promotion to chairman, potential lawsuits from the injured and insulted passenger, and most important, a loss of trust by the flying public.

The lawsuit the passenger brought against United Airlines was settled out of court, but all this grief accomplished what?

This insanity seems like a self-inflicted problem. United claimed they faced an overbooked flight requiring four passengers to be bumped. That's not true. United needed to remove four paying, already-seated customers from a full flight so four non-paying employees could shuttle a few hundred miles. United attempted to solve the problem by offering a small amount of compensation to entice people off the aircraft, which everyone rejected as insufficient. When that failed, their next step was inviting airport police aboard to remove the passengers, by force if necessary.

Problem solved, right?

The gate agents, airport police, cockpit crew, and a host of others were just following procedure. Without getting that passenger off, the aircraft couldn't push away from the gate, dinging United's on-time departure metric and likely their on-time arrival as well.

These are the "experts" of the airline industry who should know what to do.

But they didn't.

United could have put their employees in an Uber and had them to Louisville in four hours, barely longer than the time needed to get to O'Hare, pass security, board the flight, fly to Louisville, and deplane.

But that was never considered.

An airline gate supervisor could have broken the rules and paid more compensation to lure people off the plane. Paying $5,000 or even $10,000 is nothing compared to the lasting damage done to the airline by its decisions.

But that never happened.

In a *Wall Street Journal* article under the headline "United Cites Litany of Failures," United CEO Oscar Munoz called the airline's actions "a failure of epic proportions that's grown to this breach of public trust. We get that. We let our policies and procedures get in the way of doing the right thing."[6]

CEO Munoz finally wrote an open letter to the public titled "Actions Speak Louder Than Words," which appeared on the back page of the *Wall Street Journal*.[7] Some snippets:

> "We can never say we are sorry enough for the shameful way one of our customers was treated aboard United's flight 3411."

> "Corporate policies were placed ahead of our shared values."

> "Procedures got in the way of employees doing what they know is right."

> "As CEO, responsibility ultimately falls to me."

> "Meaningful actions will speak louder than words. Starting today, United is changing how we fly, serve, and respect our customers."

> "Law enforcement will not remove customers from a flight and customers will not be required to give up their seat once on board—except in matters of safety or security."

> "In case of overbooking, we will identify volunteers much earlier."

---

6   *Wall Street Journal*, April 27, 2017.
7   *Wall Street Journal*, April 27, 2017.

"We will increase incentives for voluntary re-booking up to $10,000."

"We will have a dedicated team to find other travel options for customers who give up their seat."

"We will eliminate the red tape on permanently lost bags with a new no-questions-asked $1500 reimbursement."

"We will develop new tools and training for employees to solve issues for our customers in the moment."

"We are working harder than ever for the privilege to serve you. And I know we will be a stronger, better, and more customer-focused airline as a result."

CEO Munoz summed it up: "This is a turning point for all of us at United and it signals a culture shift toward becoming a better, more customer-focused airline.... Our customers should be at the center of everything we do and these changes are just the beginning of how we will earn back their trust."

What a revelation—from a company serving nearly 150 million customers a year. You would think they were a start-up just learning the ropes.

What's still wrong with this picture? It seems like United hasn't yet addressed the fundamental overbooking issue. They've just provided more reactive remedies employees can take when a situation arises due to overbooking. In fact, an article the day after the CEO's open letter was titled "Why You Still May Get Bumped."[8]So much for the noise and drama!

Does anyone think United's fundamental policies and procedures have changed? Are there better metrics for how people will be compensated? I don't think so. Things will simply appear to be better until the next fundamental breakdown of common sense, and then the cycle of public outrage and CEO apologies will continue.

United Airlines is the poster child for why we need a Service Revolution. But there will be plenty of resistance, even after this debacle.

Existing culture runs deep, and all the metrics United depends on likely still show they have very good customer service. So why think of changing? Better to mop up the damage and move on. Yet a United that doesn't change may miss their opportunity to arrive at a different future where company values, culture, and employee actions all converge at the same point, creating a laser-beam focus on *doing the right things for the right reasons at the right time.*

By not facing the harsh reality of their behavior, United will continue marching toward extinction. They too will face disruptions, whether through fewer mega-airlines or more low-cost start-ups. Or maybe even high-speed trains and driverless cars will redefine travel. No company is guaranteed survival. A true Service Revolution is more than a feel-good tick list of incremental changes.

---

8   *Wall Street Journal,* April 28, 2017.

CASE STUDY:
Consider It Done

I traveled a lot for my job, logging well over 200,000 miles a year and staying in countless hotels. I was a global road warrior.

One bright Texas day I arrived at a 1500-room conference hotel minutes from the DFW airport. The commanding entry of the Gaylord Texan Resort & Convention Center opened to marble floors, stained woodwork, and elegant furnishings. The sparkling setting felt perfect for a service conference.

Check-in was easy and the receptionist friendly. Along with the keycard, I received a brief orientation to the massive facility. I strolled to the elevators along walkways winding among plush botanical gardens and varied restaurants. Like a mini-Disneyland without the rides!

On the eleventh floor, I found a beautiful room awaiting me. Firm bed. Plush pillows. CLEAN BATHROOM. Not like one hotel bathroom where I flipped on the lights and cockroaches scurried.

I always check the bathroom.

I emptied my suitcase into the drawers. With a three-day stay ahead, my running clothes got a separate drawer, and I couldn't wait to hit the workout room.

Then I got a sinking feeling. I hadn't packed something essential. I dug through my briefcase and each of my suitcase's zippered pockets.

No adapter for my laptop.

This was bad.

I was presenting, and my battery would never last through my presentation. I could somehow solve that. Worse, I worried about not being able to work at night. The thought of going home to hundreds of unread emails made my stomach churn.

I wasn't sure what to do. Then I saw it. The answer to my conundrum. On the nightstand, next to the phone, was a bold sign that said

CONSIDER IT DONE

I read the large placard closely. I read it three more times to make sure there was no asterisk with a string of disclaimers in tiny print. Nope. The message was unambiguous. If I had ANY problem that needed solving during my stay at this very nice hotel, I could ask and CONSIDER IT DONE!

I imagined the remedy was as easy as asking a hotel associate to dig through an accumulated mountain of laptop cords left behind by the thousands of guests who stay at the hotel every month. Surely one poor soul had left an adapter that matched my model.

I wanted the adapter before I went to bed, so I headed back down to the hotel lobby and explained my situation to the receptionist. I even quoted the CONSIDER IT DONE promise. I was told the hotel had never had this request before, and there weren't any adapters I could use.

Really? I was mostly piqued by the CONSIDER IT DONE promise. I expected a more positive response. The receptionist did recommend that I visit the customer service group when it opened at 7 a.m. the next morning.

That seemed reasonable. I saw no reason to become indignant at this point, and it was late. I was up and at the customer service desk before it opened.

The person at the customer service desk said there were no laptop adapters in their lost and found and recommended a big box store a few blocks away. Why don't I just go over and pick one up?

I held my composure. I informed the person at the service desk that—one—I had no car because I shuttled to the hotel—and two—I was booked with meetings, presentations, and appointments until late that night. I couldn't break away.

My need didn't matter. That was the best they could do.

I asked to speak to the customer service manager, who said that they could indeed run to the store for an adapter. With my faith in CONSIDER IT DONE restored, the manager agreed to call or text when the adapter was in hand.

I lost track of time. I called the customer service manager later that afternoon to inquire about my adapter. The manager responded with an "Oh, I'm sorry I haven't gotten back to you," then reported they didn't pick up the adapter because I hadn't given them a credit card. I said the hotel had my card from check-in, and they could get it there. Why did I have to explain the obvious? I suggested that if nothing else, the hotel could purchase the cord—$25?—and bill it to my room. They could add a surcharge if necessary.

The customer service manager said none of this was possible.

I was determined to prove this assertion wrong. I went back to the front desk and spoke with the front desk manager, who assured me they could, in fact, do what I wanted. I asked the front desk manager to call the customer service manager to ensure clarity of expectations. This was done.

I then went back to the customer service manager and said to please purchase the adapter and to leave it in my room. I would be working into the evening, then going out for a business dinner, and wouldn't get back to my room until late. I really needed the adapter. My battery was low, and my presentation was the next morning.

I went back to my meetings, believing my problem would be resolved—finally.

It was well after 9 p.m. when I made it back to my room.

Guess what? Nothing.

I was more disappointed than mad. When someone breaks a promise or lets you down, that's natural.

I knew the customer service desk was closed, but I walked down anyway. As fate would have it, the only person left was the hotel's operations director, who happened to be the boss of the customer service manager. Luckily, I caught him before he left, and I asked if my adapter was at customer service.

He went searching in a back room, returning after several minutes. "Is this what you're looking for?"

While I was elated to finally have my adapter, this felt like a great teachable moment. I asked the operations director if he had a few minutes for some constructive feedback.

"Certainly."

I began by saying I liked the customer service promise boldly shown in each room. CONSIDER IT DONE. I said the team ultimately met my need, but I also told the story of how a simple request required unnecessary time and attention. It felt like I—the customer—was having to connect the dots for hotel staff. Why?

I made my points calmly, one professional to another. I didn't expect the defensiveness I heard in return, with the operations director offering excuses rather than owning what happened and using it to help his entire team get better.

This story is full of important messages:

- The hotel made a great first impression and topped it off with a stunning promise: CONSIDER IT DONE.

- This unambiguous promise raised my expectations.

- The issue that needed resolution was clear and easy.

- The hotel hadn't thought through the organizational implications of their bold promise.

- Departments acted as silos.

- Individuals didn't take ownership.

- The customer had to become the problem-solver and invest too much time and energy.

- Management didn't understand the VALUE the customer promise implied.

- Management offered excuses rather than owning the issue.

- Hotel team members probably missed an opportunity to learn and get better.

- Senior leaders probably missed their opportunity to re-invent their future.

CONSIDER IT DONE felt more like CONSIDER IT DONE—OR MAYBE NOT. A decade later, my telling this story shows how even insignificant service breakdowns are hard to forget. Without intervention, they go on and on. I recently went to the Gaylord Texan website to scan reviews. Four of the eight most recent customer comments were resoundingly negative. That's 50% on the first page alone. Perhaps today's promise is CONSIDER IT DONE—NOT QUITE YET.

I tried. My teachable moment didn't stick. This hotel and senior management team—and all the people employed at this company—probably never saw the need to jumpstart their Service Revolution.

CONSIDER IT DONE is a beautiful slogan until you CAN'T. When we admit that similar failures are rampant and pervasive within our own workplaces in ways large and small, we're ready to learn what we can do about it.

What's Next

In the next chapters, we'll go deeper into the three critical dysfunctional behaviors of senior management that limit or even prevent companies from igniting the Service Revolution. These dysfunctional behaviors create such a blind spot that companies don't see the need for the Service Revolution, much like Target, United Airlines, and The Gaylord Texan Resort & Conference Center.

After probing these critical senior leader dysfunctional behaviors, the remaining chapters will focus on specific actions a company can undertake to change its DNA by catalyzing the Service Revolution. Think of these tactical means as kindling for a bonfire. The kindling burns easily, enabling larger logs to catch fire until you bask in the warmth of the roaring flames!

It's the same with jumpstarting the Service Revolution. I offer tactical suggestions that start the process until the entire organization is caught up in the action, on its way to becoming a true Service Champion—on the INSIDE with all colleagues and OUTSIDE with its end customers.

Let's grapple with those leadership dysfunctions.

CHAPTER THREE TAKEAWAYS

- The Service Revolution includes all people, functions, and groups throughout the company, particularly the company functions INSIDE the company.

- Even companies known as Service Champions develop rust on their company culture, typically from many years of experiencing dysfunctional senior leader behaviors.

- Senior leader dysfunctional behaviors manifest in company work processes, procedures, quality documents, test methods, cultural norms, performance management tools, and the individual responses.

- Dysfunctions create blind spots called "institutional disservice."

- Real-life examples of how companies who claim to be Service Leaders—and create specific customer promises—can fail the test of having a deep service culture within the company.

CHAPTER FOUR

Skip the Words,
Watch the Behaviors

"Success isn't counted by how high you've climbed but by how many people you brought with you."

WILL ROSE

A good friend of mine is a world-class strategic planning consultant. I worked with Dr. Lou Mahigel at Emerson Electric when we needed assistance conducting strategic planning for our large field organization.

It was Lou who coined the saying "Skip the words, watch the behaviors." When I first heard the statement, it bounced off me. I have my own blind spots, and one is a tendency to be overly trusting. I expect people to show up authentically, as people who "say what they do and do what they say."

The more time I spent with Lou and pondered his words, sure enough, I began to see disconnects between what people said and what they did. I saw that it was particularly prevalent among senior leaders.

My ah-ha moment was this. I came to believe that many senior leaders consciously say one thing and do another.

It took a while for that to sink in too. It still makes me shudder.

Is it possible that some senior leaders—for whatever their noble purpose—would say one thing in a senior leadership meeting, then exit and do the opposite? And routinely repeat this behavior?

You might assume such egregious distortion and deception can't go on. People will see the disconnect, and the offender will get caught in their lies.

Will they?

I've peered into enough senior leadership teams in enough companies to tell you this behavior by senior leaders is real. Sometimes rampant. And it always seems to be tolerated.

How can this be?

Let's consider a few real-life actual examples of this senior leader dysfunctional behavior number one, saying one thing and doing another.

Senior Leader Dysfunctional Behavior Number One: Saying One Thing and Doing Another

Example One: The cultural paradox

This is big—so we're covering it first. Not all senior leaders are dishonest. They aren't the only people in an organization with this dissembling shortcoming. I've observed this phenomenon up and down organizations, from frontlines to boardrooms.

The focus here is on dysfunctional behaviors of senior leadership because they ultimately control the organization. They decide whether programs get approved or axed. Who moves up and who moves out. Who gets a raise and who goes home disheartened. Not to mention which budgets grow while others get decimated. They choose the company goals that move to the top this year and the next and beyond. Most important, senior leaders guard the gateway to the company's culture, values, and norms. In the end, they're the ones who build trust or its opposite, mistrust and fear.

I'm amazed by the seeming lack of understanding of the critical role senior leaders play in evolving a company's culture.

Here is where I see a real paradox.

I've concluded that senior leaders intellectually grasp their role in their company's culture. But culture isn't intellectual. It's emotional. It's how people react in their gut to the company and what it stands for. Do people *believe* they can trust senior management? Do they *feel* their leaders care about their career development? Do they *respect* the boss who surprises them at a performance review with "meets expectations" when they deserve "exceeds expectations"? And what are they supposed to *think* when someone in another department does the same work and quality but gets the "exceeds expectations"?

The words "believe," "feel," "respect," and "think" are all rooted more in emotional feeling than intellectual reality.

The paradox is that management can do all kinds of right things to improve the culture, like workshops on trust, town halls where people can voice questions and concerns, or skip-level meetings to facilitate interaction between people up and down the org chart.

All good things. But if a senior management team that hasn't developed a culture of trust, eliminated fear in the workplace, and created cross-company equity for performance reviews and merit increases, then all their good deeds won't leave a lasting positive impact on the company, the people who work there, or the culture everyone lives in.

Example Two: New products are king!

Most companies set aggressive goals for developing and launching new products, with senior management calling new products "the lifeblood of the company." Leaders set specific goals for the number of new products to be launched per year, along with anticipated net revenue and percentage of total revenue. The higher the percentage, the greater the perception the company is innovating. The lower the percentage, well, something is wrong.

At one company I've observed at length, senior leadership spoke endlessly about the need for new products, but you would never know they meant it by watching their behaviors.

Senior management wanted 10 or more new product launches per year, a gargantuan task for a small group of engineers and a handful of techs in the test lab. When anyone argued that the goal was unattainable, senior management replied that "The goal is the goal" and that "Good leaders find a way to make it happen."

I can buy that. Challenges build an organization's character. Except when the goals ARE impossible, and senior management gives lip service to supporting them. Worse yet is when they pile on shame and blame. Everyone on the receiving end feels bewildered, frustrated, and resentful of senior leadership that doesn't walk the talk.

Here's where it got concrete. Senior leadership wouldn't get at the chaos the Quality Department was creating around new product launches. The group was dedicated to compliance, not new product development, resulting in long delays in getting critical documents reviewed, approved, and signed off. Testing couldn't start until the documents cleared, with delays happening day-after-day and many projects stalling for weeks and even months.

Engineering continually raised the issue with Quality to no avail, a department which, by the way, was a ghost town by 4 p.m. most afternoons.

In bi-weekly project reviews, senior management pointed to the date slippage and demanded to know what the project manager was doing to "bring the dates back in"! Project managers reported that getting documents signed was the cause of almost all the delays. Rather than address this issue with Quality, the issue was skirted and the project manager flapped in the wind with no way to resolve the problem.

Even when the Quality team was given resources by Engineering, hiring several contractors to tackle the workload, the focus on compliance stuck. Why wouldn't it? That's how the group was measured and compensated!

Senior management would toss out the usual platitudes. "We should do a better job of prioritizing documents." Or "Blame Engineering. They had too many deliverables due at the same time." (That's what happens when work doesn't get done but dates go unchanged.)

Senior management's ultimate answer was that Engineering needed to collaborate better with the Quality Department. There was no candid discussion that:

- Quality marched to a different drummer than Engineering, despite senior management's belief that the company was all aligned around common goals.

- Quality didn't have the same urgency about new product deliverables as Engineering.

- New product delays were PREDICTABLE given senior management's behavior.

To add insult to injury, as in most companies, Finance measured and reported Engineering/R&D expenses as a percentage of sales. The Quality Department's expenses were included but unnoted in Engineering/R&D numbers, creating a glaring budget overshoot. The budget "overrun" was an accounting hitch, but Engineering nevertheless caught the blame. Moreover, because Quality had hired multiple contractors to manage compliance, the expenses on the Engineering/R&D line on the P&L ballooned. The impact? Engineering was asked to cut its budget.

Let's recap.

- Senior management continually preached new products as the lifeblood of the company.

- Challenging new product launch goals were set— challenging indeed, given the small Engineering group.

- New product delays were common and almost always related to slowness in signing off documents.

- Senior leaders approved unrealistic deadlines, yet chastised the project manager when dates came and went.

- Quality got away with disregarding launch schedules, despite corporate goals calling that out as a key priority for every department.

- The Engineering budget was chopped because "We're not seeing results for all the money we spend on engineering," even though the overruns were an accounting quirk, an obvious fact that senior leaders dismissed.

- And the final *coup de grace?* When performance reviews rolled around, the Quality team received far higher performance ratings and merit compensation than their peers in Engineering.

You can't make this stuff up. There are times when truth is stranger than fiction. And new products continue to be a struggle for this company.

What made the situation even more astonishing was that managers and front-line folks all understood what was going on. Every two weeks they had to stand in front of management and explain why dates continued to slip. Their feedback was always the same: inability to get documents signed off on a timely basis, misaligned priorities between departments, and senior management setting too many "number one priorities."

With truth set before senior leaders like a choice steak, they refused to take in and digest the real problem.

So much for one set of company goals, one laser-beam focus from all departments on top company priorities, and one aligned senior leadership team building trust and collaboration into the DNA of the company's culture.

Lou was right: "Skip the words and watch the behaviors."

Example Three: The critical spare parts will get here—after 60 days!

At a past company, we had won a major contract with one of our largest customers, securing the service agreement by making no-nonsense guarantees of product up-time. Senior management signed off on the proposal with a clear understanding of the deal's implications. Our excellent delivery record made the risks—which were significant—feel manageable.

The contract commitments were so large they took more than three months to implement fully. People had to be hired, trained, and deployed. We also chose to audit all field equipment covered under the new contract to ensure we were on top of any potential risks, particularly continued servicing of some rather ancient equipment.

What happened next is another textbook example of the dysfunctional senior leader behavior of saying one thing and doing another.

Over time, we found the consumption of expensive spare parts was far greater than predicted. We isolated the high parts usage to a piece of equipment present in hundreds of customer facilities across the U.S. and Canada. While this equipment saw heavy use and parts were prone to wear, the absolute number and cost seemed excessive. But this was our largest customer, and we had signed a service contract that included all necessary parts.

With usage so high, we started to run out of parts. The solution was to buy more spares, which we did. The equipment and parts were produced in a factory overseas, and we flew critical spare parts from the factory to our warehouse for eventual use by our field service techs.

Keep in mind that we had guaranteed specific up-times with this major customer. As we started to run out of spare parts, we ran headfirst into these promises. This was bad. If the equipment was down, our customer couldn't complete jobs. No finished jobs, no revenue for our customer. Through no fault of their own.

We started flying in even more spare parts.

Then reality struck. The company where I worked aimed to reduce costs. They settled on inbound freight as the first cut. An immediate ban on air shipments required all the equipment and parts we needed arrive by ocean freight. The prohibition meant A 60-DAY WAIT FOR PARTS—MINIMUM! Combine that mandate with an uptime guarantee measured in hours and days—not weeks and months—and we had a crash-and-burn business disaster just around the corner.

I should make clear it wasn't just spare parts being air-shipped to our warehouse. Equipment was as well. In fact, a PARETO chart on air freight costs showed equipment was the worst offender—high inbound freight costs—not the spare parts.

That said, the new policy went forward. When I asked for a waiver on critical spare parts, I was told to plan better.

I have no problem with better forecasting. But in a do-or-die window with equipment down at a major customer and us facing fines for missing up-time guarantees, getting spare parts to our warehouse ASAP seemed to be common sense. We agreed to specific guarantees, but now we couldn't get parts we needed to meet them.

By the way, the SVP who nixed air freighting of critical parts was the same SVP who signed off on the major contract that included up-time guarantees. I thought again of my friend Lou. WATCH THE BEHAVIORS! I was face-to-face with senior leadership saying one thing and doing another.

Don't get me wrong. We had real issues we needed to fix, among them this spare parts issue. By then we had learned that customer operators were carelessly damaging spare parts, openly musing that "It didn't matter because the service company has to replace these parts for free." Many of those parts cost a few hundred dollars—each!

We had all agreed to this contract. Other costs could be cut. But none of that mattered. Senior leadership dug in on this cost-cutting "fix."

I can't begin to quantify the trust we lost. The end customer was furious about the downtime and loss of business. Our service techs were frustrated because they couldn't complete repairs and keep customers happy. And the home office team lost faith in the senior management, who threw up roadblocks rather than help solve a serious problem.

Your World

Have you experienced a senior leader who said one thing and did another?

I thought so. I knew I wasn't alone.

How did that leader's behavior impact your ability to do your job and serve the internal and external customers?

How equipped were you to meet the goals on which you would be compensated at year-end?

When you encountered a problem that needed fixing, what disconnects did you observe between management directions and the dictates of common sense?

What was the ultimate impact on your company's culture? On trust? Communication? And performance management?

My guess is that trust was broken in a big way, and the end customer felt the pain.

In the next chapter, we'll address another critical dysfunctional behavior of senior leaders that creates mistrust and keeps companies from jumpstarting the Service Revolution.

CHAPTER FOUR TAKEAWAYS

- "Skip the words, watch the behaviors" enables employees to sniff out dysfunctional senior leader behaviors.

- This chapter highlighted the dysfunctional behavior of "saying one thing and doing another."

- Real life examples of this behavior in action included:

  - The cultural paradox

  - New products are king

  - Critical spare parts

- Trust is broken and nobody wins.

  - Customers get upset at the company.

  - Front-line employees become frustrated because they can't serve their customers.

  - Team members at the home office lose faith in senior management.

CHAPTER FIVE

Care You Show vs. Show You Care

"The best gift you can give is encouragement. Yet almost no one gets the encouragement they need to grow to their full potential. If everyone received the encouragement they need to grow, genius would blossom and produce abundance beyond our dreams."

SIDNEY MADWED

Senior leader dysfunctional behavior number two is really a subset of first misbehavior, saying one thing and doing another. I break out this behavior and cover it in depth because it's so critical to measuring the health of any company as well as the trust employees have in senior management.

The phrase "care you show vs. show you care" distinguishes between the empty words and playacting often seen from senior leaders versus authentic demonstrations of care.

One manager stands out. She wanted to be sure her people noticed the care she showed in a group meeting. By providing recognition or acknowledging a success, she checked the care box on her to-do list in a way everyone could see.

Yet no one among her direct reports or large division felt she cared. She never asked about their families or life outside of work or what she could do to make someone's job better. People felt zero true empathy. Everything was about her.

I see this paradox in many senior leaders. They go out of their way to ensure you're aware of "the care they show" to others, but as the receiver of this care, YOU NEVER FELT THEM "SHOW THEY REALLY CARE." It's all an act.

If senior leaders aren't genuine and don't demonstrate actual care for their people and work teams, it really doesn't matter how much care they show. Their lack of authenticity breeds cynicism and poor employee engagement.

My choice of words for this senior leader dysfunctional be-havior number two is a spin on words credited to Theodore Roosevelt. To paraphrase, he said, "People don't care how much you know until they know how much you care."

Isn't that the truth! How often have you heard a leader say all the right things even as a gnawing feeling in your gut tells you they don't mean it? Not deep down. Not with the kind of real-world proof that wins your heart and inspires you to want to follow.

Oddly, the senior leader doing the talking thinks they're sin-cere. You might be at a town hall or a company-sponsored event or even a one-on-one. The words all sound good—heck—even the PowerPoint deck has some cool graphics. But it just doesn't feel right. The vibe hits you as hollow, like the person spouting off doesn't care as much as they claim. (Hence the tight connection with the last chapter's dysfunction: Skip the words, watch the behaviors!)

Let me give you some real-life examples of this type of dysfunctional behavior, "care you show vs. show you care."

Senior Leader Dysfunctional Behavior Number Two:
Care You Show vs. Show You Care

Example One: The annual performance review

I can think of few things that have become more unrewarding than the annual performance review. I admit my contribution to this problem. For all the years I was on the giving end of performance reviews, you can bet I tried my best to be present and authentic. I tried hard to shut my mouth and give my employees a platform to speak. That said, God knows I could have done a better job!

When I was the employee being reviewed, I felt unease inside. Watching other senior leaders conduct performance reviews or hearing about their practices secondhand only heightened a surreal feeling. I came to believe that reviews are a largely pointless exchange that merely sets up a discussion of merit compensation and possible raises. "Tell me about the money," we mutter to ourselves, "and let me out of here."

My point here might not be what you expect. Sure, I'm con-
cerned about bosses who use performance reviews to savage
employees. Or those who bring up performance concerns that
should have been raised and resolved long ago. But I've concluded that a far more powerful human dynamic undercuts
the whole exchange. The performance review, no matter how
good or bad in the moment, in the end doesn't matter much.
Why? Because we're seldom convinced our bosses care.

Of course, leaders say they care, but that's why I raise this
as a critical dysfunctional behavior senior leaders must address before serious transformational change can occur in an
organization.

Think about your last few annual performance reviews. Did
your boss regurgitate verbatim the list of accomplishments
and improvement areas you submitted in preparation for your
review? Or did your boss rely mostly on peer feedback, stitching the input into a document that feels as if it was written
about somebody else—not you?

Or how about the boss who tosses your input? You get the feeling their mind was made up long ago. In fact, many companies
demand preliminary employee ratings be submitted months
ahead of reviews so merit compensation dollars can be bud-
geted. But preliminary ratings have a funny way of hardening
into today's reality. You could have done heroic work in the
last six months, but your annual rating was already booked!

Does any of this make you feel valued? How much trust is lost
through a process like that? Keep in mind these same senior
leaders demand stronger cross-functional collaboration while
they exhibit behavior that seems cold and one-sided.

Most employees eventually learn to shut out whatever they hear in their reviews. They're just putting up with whatever comes until their boss gets to the bottom line.

From the other side of the desk, the annual performance review is about nothing more than senior leaders vying for their share of a company's compensation dollars. The better the ratings, the more compensation money can be given out to their group, particularly to those deemed high performers. If you're not in that circle, you either get a glowing review with lower compensation— a real air-biscuit—or a so-so review and still lower merit dollars.

In any case, your experience is that the senior leaders never really took the time to listen and communicate effectively at your review. You, the employee, never felt your leader showing real care.

Is it any wonder GE ditched the annual performance review? Or any surprise a company's culture is so hard to change? Can you see the difficulty of jumpstarting the Service Revolution when there's no spark among the workforce?

Example Two: The employee engagement survey— or is it disengagement?

At every company where I worked and was a senior leader, the issue of improving employee engagement was a big deal. It made the list of top company priorities year after year. And for good reason. Who wants an employee base that is disengaged?

From my perspective, it seemed more like a beauty contest than something vital that should command the attention of senior leaders.

For example, at one company we conducted annual employee engagement surveys via a web-based survey tool. The senior leadership claimed absolute anonymity of the survey respondents, but the first five questions drilled down on geography, division, function, even the name of your boss! The only thing missing? Typing your email address twice to create an account.

But here's the profound point. Even though the percentage of respondents wasn't as high as expected—*hmmm*—the ratings were atrocious. Company-wide employee engagement averaged less than 55%. Only with a score of 80% could a senior leadership team feel they were doing well.

Even more amazing was the lack of follow-up on the results to truly improve the outcome. Teams formed, and initiatives kicked off, but urgency and purpose at improving results were usually lacking.

Then another year rolled by and another engagement survey was conducted. This time the questions were different so that you couldn't get a true year-over-year comparison and gauge improvement. It was like starting over. But everyone celebrated that our employee engagement had risen to 62%. Wow! Only 18 percentage points until we hit "good."

This cycle continued: Conduct survey, get results that weren't so hot, say we need to improve, establish some new actions. Repeat cycle.

What struck me the most was the vivid display of senior leaders lining up with "care they show" about this important issue but never really "showing they care." When leaders don't demonstrate care, it's hard to trust them with your future. And what if that future is the need to jumpstart the Service Revolution?

Senior leaders and their behaviors hold the keys to unlocking the energy and enthusiasm to change an outcome. To change the future. To begin to change the culture. But without showing you care about people or a compelling future you can seek together, then it's all a mirage.

Here's some additional proof the "employee engagement" is an issue, and that the boss is usually at the heart of the problem. Consider this nugget from the *Wall Street Journal* on how some toxic bosses manage to hang on to their jobs:

> Many people have found themselves working for a nightmare boss at some point, and according to a 2015 Gallup Study of 7200 U.S. adults, half of the workers have left at least one job because of a bad manager. But the Life Meets Work survey suggests that working for an abusive or dysfunctional supervisor is even more commonplace: Among those polled, 56% described their current manager as toxic.[9]

Wow! Over half of all workers think their boss is toxic. Not just unpleasant, unfriendly, or un-something but TOXIC!

If we're ever to have a high degree of positive employee engagement—a critical factor in achieving transformational organizational change—then senior leaders need to wake up to this issue.

---

9   *Wall Street Journal,* May 31, 2017.

Example Three: Onboarding
(better known as "you're on your own!")

Isn't it amazing? Company values plaster the walls. The mission statement avows that "People are our most valued asset." We spend big dollars and equally precious leader time recruiting top talent.

The process usually involves multiple candidates for a position. Eventually, a candidate wins, and an offer appears. When the candidate accepts, the hiring manager and others express excitement and anticipation of good things to come. A candidate gives at least a couple weeks' notice. But time flies, and before you know it, the new hire arrives in the front lobby!

The hiring manager or Human Resources picks up the new employee and likely does a few introductions on the way back to the work area.

Then reality sets in.

The new employee learns where he or she will sit, over yonder in the cube farm or maybe an individual office. But something is missing. Oh—IT hasn't gotten around to setting up the new person's office computer, and so all of those "Welcome Aboard!" emails from around the company just lie dormant. And the phone isn't set up. Other than a desk and chair, little has been prepared in advance for the newbie we were so glad to hire. So the new person gets a stack of material to read and the boss swings by to say we'll do more introductions and start the onboarding process later in the day.

I'm not joking. More than once I've seen this is the norm. A couple of new colleagues tied for a record, waiting six weeks before they scored a computer. SIX WEEKS!

Despite the pleading of the department head to accelerate the process, nothing was resolved. Now let's throw in a little circular logic.

Imagine a new employee has his login information. Just no computer to log into. In a burst of creative problem-solving, the department head instructs the new employee to log into his email account using another employee's computer.

That brings down cataclysmic hail and fury. You would think the world is ending. IT policy prohibits anyone from logging into email using another person's computer. No exceptions!

Never mind it's been six weeks. The department head tries again, handing the new guy an underutilized loaner computer, a move that also turns out to be a big no-no. IT policy bans unassigned loaners from being used for office functions, meaning no email access. No exceptions!

Around the holidays, the office has a decorating contest. The new guy's department outfits its area to look like Santa's workshop, complete with a jumbo-sized wish list. At the top of the list? A computer for the new hire. The GM admires the department's clever decorations and laughs at the list. Until he finds out the top item is for real. Only because he inserts himself into the logjam does the employee get a computer.

SIX WEEKS!

What impression do you suppose this employee formed during his onboarding experience? No phone or computer on day one. No easy way to get and fill out forms. No access to critical files he needs to do the job the company was so eager to fill. No formal or even informal onboarding process. No new employee training. Just a quick meet and greet with the team followed by sequestering with a mound of reading because there was nothing else to do. Ouch!

How can senior leaders hope to win the hearts and minds of work teams if the people we bring in feel devalued from the start, all because there was no preparation to properly onboard the new employee? It's like forgetting your partner's birthday—or your anniversary. If you've been there, you know the feeling. It's awful. And it should be.

Remember the sign in front said that "People are our most valued asset"? What happened between that sign on the lobby wall and reality back in the office area? And what is the impact to the company? Everyone talks. People crack light-hearted jokes. And what gets ingrained in the company's psyche is that senior leadership talks a good game of caring for its employees, but they never show they really care.

Example Four: Career development— how do I get ahead?

My final example of senior leaders exhibiting the dysfunctional behavior of "care you show vs. show you care" is about career development.

To work for a company that cares about their professional development tops the list of most millennials. I think most everyone, regardless of age, job responsibility, company, or industry cares about their future development. Job advancement, learning new skills, experiencing a variety of management styles, getting an opportunity for a higher income—all drive what people think when they hear "career development."

I point to millennials as an example because I've observed that as a group, they're more acutely aware of their own desire for tangible development at work. Millennials voice a larger goal of improving society—not just themselves—and growing at work is an important step in the journey.

And really—how can career development be anything but a good thing for the company? Employees who want to develop themselves by experiencing new jobs or new assignments, in the process making themselves more valuable, are far more likely to be considered for future leadership roles as part of every company's succession planning.

But here's the rub.

Most companies I've observed that preach career planning have nothing behind the curtain. It was just two words. Career. Planning. For the employee, it was mostly DIY, Do It Yourself. Employees asked about gaining additional experience in another part of the company, but nothing ever transpired. To be fair, with companies running lean it's difficult to give up an employee and give them alternate experiences.

But the result of this continued lack of progress or even honest effort to assist an employee with career development means they eventually stop investing themselves in the company. Their creativity goes elsewhere as they expend discretionary time and energy in causes outside the company. They "quit and stay," showing up for work but withholding their best. Or they leave for another job just to get the learning experiences they crave.

What about the company that loses that employee? It's tough. They poured time and effort into on-the-job training for the employee, and they were doing great work. And now there's an organizational hole to fill.

It's sad. Nobody wins. Well, the employee gets the new experience they wanted, but at the expense of giving up their old job, leaving their co-workers and friends, maybe even sacrificing a future promotion and increased compensation at their old company.

And for what? Who says the new company's career development process is any different? I bet that it isn't. Here we see again a huge missed opportunity for senior leadership to show they care.

In the next chapter, we'll address one final critical dysfunctional behavior of senior leaders that prevents companies from jumpstarting the Service Revolution.

CHAPTER FIVE TAKEAWAYS

- Senior leader dysfunctional behavior number two is "Care you show vs. show you care."

- This behavior is of critical personal importance to individual employees.

- Real-life examples of this dysfunctional senior leader behavior include:

  - The annual performance review

  - The employee engagement survey

  - Onboarding

  - Career development

- The impact of this dysfunctional behavior is that employees quit and leave. Or worse yet, they quit and stay, meaning you lose their creativity and get none of their discretionary time.

CHAPTER SIX

When Everything Is a Priority, Nothing Is a Priority

"Nothing can add more power to your life than concentrating all your energies on a limited set of targets."

NIDO QUBEIN

Give me a show of hands. Have you ever felt your company has one too many "number one priorities," with multiple, sometimes conflicting priorities cascading down to your annual performance plan?

No, you're not allowed to raise more than two hands.

What amazes me is the universality of this issue. Senior leader critical dysfunction number one runs rampant, "Saying one thing and doing another." More than likely you've been witness to dysfunction number two, "Care you show vs. show you care."

But no organization on earth ever escapes dysfunction number three, "When everything is a priority, nothing is a priority!"

Every company I've worked at has suffered from an advanced case of this disease. It didn't matter if we were on a fast-track growth path or struggling to meet our objectives. The company's goals were many-fold. Too many-fold!

When I was little, my mother always told me to only put on my plate the amount of food I was going to eat. And when I didn't heed her words, and dinner was over, and yes, there was still food on my plate, she looked at me as only my mother could and said, "I guess your eyes were bigger than your stomach."

Despite lots of little boys and girls hearing that advice, as leaders, we all grew up to think we know better.

And this better way is omnipresent!

The process starts with the annual update of the three- to five-year strategic plan. Most companies have given up trying to see five years into the future, so they make do with a three-year strategic vision. I still think planning out longer is better, especially when you consider the technological and social disruptions changing the landscape across multiple industries. Strategic planning can't be an exercise in linear forecasting, as in "Tomorrow will be just like today—only a little bigger and better."

Instead, by jumpstarting the Service Revolution, the metrics around what you do to advance the future of the company can be dramatically different.

I'm getting ahead of myself.

Today we have senior leadership teams setting goals and objectives for the company to achieve during the fiscal year. The goals often appear pretty lofty, covering company-wide financial objectives as well as objectives for each major area, including Engineering/R&D, Manufacturing/Supply Chain, Sales and Marketing, Quality, IT, and Human Resources. Each department has top-level goals that cascade into even more granular objectives for employees in each department. It wouldn't be uncommon to have five major goal headings, each with five top-level objectives. Before long, you have 25 key things for the organization to achieve in a given year.

At one organization, we strove to get this number down to JUST 10 to 12 objectives for the year. How did we do this? Were we just amazing prioritizers?

Nope. We got there by wordsmithing several objectives together. You can try it for yourself:

> Key objective: Achieve 10% growth in North America AND introduce five new products AND reduce sales costs by 5% AND ensure voluntary employee turnover doesn't exceed 4%.

Bingo! Four objectives molded into one. Were we good or what?

We all had a good laugh about this and named the process after one of the senior leaders, an individual so prolific at stitching together multiple objectives that we turned his name into a verb. I can't share it here. I want to keep these dear people as friends. But I can tell you that our word describing this phenomenon was clever and catchy.

I really wish I could tell you.

With our list of dozens of objectives compacted, we proudly launched each year with just a handful of things to get done, while the real number of objectives we all signed up to achieve amounted to a 5X multiple. Front-line leaders and their teams were frustrated by the amount of real work the senior leaders threw their way. More problematic was the game-playing that erupted behind the scenes, with senior leaders working to limit the number of objectives their team had responsibility for by shifting them to other leaders and groups.

Great teamwork. Really strong alignment among the leadership team. Not!

On the surface, at least, all the senior leaders participated in the exercise of planning. At the department level, especially where cross-functional collaboration is critical, things fell apart. Lack of trust, infighting, and resource battles were the reality.

Here again, we see the unintended consequences of poor senior leadership behavior. Leaders thought they were being clever and patted themselves on the back for how smart they were to structure such ambitious goals and objectives. But employees felt disillusioned, worried about getting a "partially meets" rating at the all-important annual review. They knew their team struggled just to stay in place, much less make real progress.

When employees are in this frame of mind, how can they be expected to go above and beyond?

Another miserable outcome of too many number one priorities is how teams and individuals get torn asunder each time management jumps on a different priority horse. What you thought was the right direction (you knew your priorities and were working on them) suddenly shifts headings (you thought we were going left, and now it's "Go right!"). Key quarterly items suddenly drop in priority. Managers direct everyone to shift their efforts to a different "urgent" item that "must be addressed."

Most problematic on a personal level, there is unlikely any discussion about updating your performance plan to reflect this new slate of objectives. A sinking feeling hits you that these new key objectives are an AND function. Meaning you get to do them AND everything else already on the docket.

In the long run, this behavior erodes trust in management, diminishes employee engagement, and sends the likelihood of missed opportunities and improvements soaring. When senior leadership goes on a tear to complete tasks, the "vision thing" loses. There's no will-power among working teams to explore and create.

Ironically, the senior leaders are all revved up. They're checking off boxes, slaying the dragon, making big things occur.

It's all an illusion.

Listen to the language senior leaders use to describe their terrific successes, clichés they forbid subordinates to use because they don't tell you anything concrete about achieving the goal— or not. But senior leaders use it all the time. No doubt you've heard the same jargon in your company as well. You hear:

- "We're **making progress** on this important objective."

- "We've **narrowed the gap** on our out-of-tolerance control parameters."

- "The **leverage we are getting** from this action is terrific."

- "We **now have a good first draft** of our new product portfolio."

- "We are **gaining steam on implementing** this new program."

- "We are **using a very proactive approach** to solving this issue."

- "We've **delivered significant progress** on our strategic restructuring program."

Say what?

Nobody falls for this management-speak when they need concrete and substantive details. The long faces and silence you see in town halls, especially when NO ONE says anything during the Q&A afterward, provide a true picture of what employees think. And it's not about what more THEY can do.

Try This Test

Here's a test I use. Everywhere I've rolled out this simple test, people have been unable to answer it uniformly or even correctly.

This awkward outcome isn't an indictment of people answering the question, nor a reflection of their abilities or commitment to doing their job well. They just don't know. Their leaders never really properly communicated with them.

Here's the test. Ask an assortment of people across the different groups, functions, and departments of your company this question:

WHAT ARE THE TOP THREE PRIORITIES OF OUR COMPANY?

It's simple. But I've yet to get a consistent response in any company where I've asked employees this question. I've asked the same of senior leaders and gotten only marginally better results.

This outcome is surprising, given the diligence of senior leaders in setting annual goals and objectives for the company and their amazing follow-on rigor of cascading goals and objectives into performance planning documents for all employees, word-smithing notwithstanding.

So how could anyone still be confused about top company goals?

Well, when you go around and ask people, you get a buffet of interesting answers. But never anything resembling a cohesively-led team where everyone in the company knows the top company priorities.

Don't believe me? Try it.

My observations tell me senior leaders spend so much time in the corner conference room—literally talking to themselves—that they simply grossly underestimate what it takes for their teams and company employees to understand, internalize, repeat, and believe THE TOP COMPANY PRIORITIES.

The problem is aggravated by the fact that even many senior leadership teams can't recite the top three company priorities.

Some get the goals and objectives right but not their priority order. Some can't do either.

With a heap of annual goals and objectives, and priorities shifting quarterly, even monthly and weekly, is it any wonder employees can't keep it straight? I know I couldn't.

While it surely may be counterintuitive, I think the best approach for most companies is to truly focus on the TOP THREE company priorities, highlighting these as the priorities of EVERYONE IN THE COMPANY.

Skeptics will say this is too simplistic. Companies are global, with multiple divisions and structures, and therefore are a more complex environment for setting goals and objectives.

This is true. But I would submit that is more of an excuse than a reason.

What good does it do to have a set of goals and objectives people don't understand, don't buy into, and can't even repeat? Moreover, shouldn't all companies KPIs (Key Performance Indicators) revolve around three basic things—cost, revenue, and customer loyalty? If these are the critical KPIs, then working backward, every company should be able to align their top three company goals and objectives to their own specific KPIs.

From there, each employee's specific work deliverables vary. But they're tightly bound to the top three company priorities. People have a hard time remembering when the number of important things they must accomplish exceeds three. There are exceptions, but not many.

And now for the MOST IMPORTANT REASON to focus on the top three company priorities rather than a senior leader laundry list of goals and objectives: How else do we expect our employees to have the time and mindset to be able to see the disruptions impacting their company and industries? And not just disruptions occurring today but those just around the corner?

If we're sure of no other fact in business, it's this: Nothing is immune to dramatic change. As Theodore Levitt wrote in one of his famous *Harvard Business Review* articles, "The history of every dead and dying 'growth' industry shows a self-deceiving cycle of bountiful expansion and undetected decay."

Levitt wrote those words in 1960.

The seeds of eventual "decay," as Levitt puts it, are sown in a company's FAILURE to focus on what is most important. FAILURE to keep priorities simple so all employees can understand, repeat, and believe them. FAILURE to align senior leaders so there is no daylight between departmental and company top goals. And FAILURE of senior leaders to practice the right behaviors that enable those who see the disruption coming to have a voice in the transformational change that is required.

Who are the modern-day Paul Reveres in your company? Are you listening to what they're saying? Do you hear their calls for action?

Are your employees thinking about what the company's products and services will be in the next five years—and how your go-to-market strategy will drastically change? Or are they thinking about what's for lunch—and punching out early today?

Of all the senior leader dysfunctional behaviors we have discussed, this is the most pervasive and persistent. It's the one senior leaders could correct, if only they knew where to start.

I submit that all transformational change requires a huge cultural shift within the organization.

I also submit that the key to getting the right culture in place is to jumpstart the Service Revolution in your company.

By doing that, these top three senior leader dysfunctional behaviors that we have covered can be banished, replaced by much stronger service-centered, customer-centric behaviors that will serve the entire organization in a profoundly better way.

CHAPTER SIX TAKEAWAYS

- The third and final senior leader dysfunctional behavior is "When everything is a priority, nothing is a priority."

- Senior leaders rationalize accepting far too many goals and objectives to achieve during a fiscal year.

- This problem is compounded by additional priorities popping up and getting assigned, with little or no relief from the initial objectives.

- Shifting priorities lead to confusion among employees about what's really important as well as exhaustion caused by trying to tackle too much in a given quarter.

- A good test is to individually ask employees from across departments and functions this question: What are the top three priorities of our company?

- Hint: Ask senior leaders as well. You'll be surprised by the lack of a consistent answer.

- Employees and leaders must have time to think, plan, and create the future-state as their industry faces disruption.

CHAPTER SEVEN

The Senior Leader- Employee Gulf

"A boss creates fear, a leader confidence.
A boss fixes blame, a leader corrects mistakes.
A boss knows all, a leader asks questions.
A boss makes work drudgery,
a leader makes it interesting.
A boss is interested in himself or herself,
a leader is interested in the group."

RUSSELL EWING

Before we move into the next chapter, examining what it takes for companies to accomplish transformational changes, I want to summarize two outlooks that exist side-by-side in almost every company, specifically, the perspective of senior leaders compared to the perspective of employees. My list detailing these outlooks isn't comprehensive. There are inevitably exceptions, with not every leader or every employee answering exactly as I spell out.

The relevant point is this: A cavernous gulf exists between what senior leaders think and believe to be true—and what employees see, feel, and believe.

Bridging this gap is critical.

We've seen throughout this book how companies failed to evolve their way of doing business as disruptive changes ravaged their industry. We've also highlighted that in most cases companies were simply not ready to make necessary changes, even when there were perceptive people within the company that saw a freight train of disruption barreling toward them.

My fundamental premise is that certain senior leader dysfunctional behaviors are at the root of this organizational paralysis to change. And in most cases, senior leaders are oblivious to their negative impact on their employees. What senior leaders see and believe isn't what employees see and believe.

To amplify this point, let's look at a recent study published by Brian Solis and Jerome Buvat at CapGemini titled "The Digital Culture Challenge: Closing the Employee-Leadership Gap."[10] Their study consists of interviews with 1700 senior-level executives and employees in 340 organizations across eight countries. I chose to include this study because of the key parallels between the culture needed to advance digital transformation in companies and industries which are or will be experiencing disruption and the cultural elements essential to establish a service-centered, customer-centric culture—the all-important by-product of a successful Service Revolution.

---

10 Brian Solis and Jerome Buvat, *The Digital Culture Challenge: Closing the Employee-Leadership Gap* (Paris: Capgemini, 2017).

The purpose of the study was to determine if these organizations had a "digital culture" necessary for achieving the disruptive digital transformation occurring within several industries. In this study, this digital culture has seven key attributes:

1. Innovation

2. Data-Driven Decision Making

3. Collaboration

4. Open Culture

5. Digital First Mindset

6. Agility and Flexibility

7. Customer-Centricity

What I find amazing but not surprising is the gulf between what senior leaders believe about their company's strength in these attributes vs. what the employees think.

Here are a few examples directly quoted from the study:

"We easily collaborate across functions and business units."
Survey Results: Leaders: 85%, Employees: 41%

"My organization has a culture of promoting collaboration and exchange of ideas across different departments and functions."
Survey Results: Leadership: 95%, Employees: 52%

"We have a culture of innovation,
experimentation, and risk-taking."
Survey Results: Leaders: 75%, Employees: 37%

"We have a culture of openness to the outside world.
We work closely with start-ups and partners."
Survey Results: Leaders: 65%, Employees: 34%

"My organization has a culture
of flexibility and agility."
Survey Results: Leaders: 56%; Employees: 40%

"Leadership acts as role models in displaying
openness to change and adopting new behaviors."
Survey Results: Leaders: 71%, Employees: 41%

"Redesigned company core values to
include digital culture attributes."
Survey Results: Leaders: 65%, Employees: 46%

"Organization has a digital vision which is
well communicated through the company."
Survey Results: Leaders: 61%, Employees: 40%

What's the common theme in these questions and results? It's the huge gap between what senior leaders believe to be true and what employees feel and believe.

Senior leaders need to confront their own dysfunctional behaviors that create this gap and be purposeful about making real changes, starting with the top three senior leadership dysfunctions we have discussed. For their part, employees need to shed their passivity and be real change agents in their own companies.

To be clear, it's unrealistic to expect employees to lead change if senior leadership doesn't first address its own dysfunctional behaviors. And change won't happen overnight. Culture changes—especially transformational changes—take years to bring about.

But there simply is NO alternative. I guess companies could invoke the old saying that "Survival is optional," meaning companies can overtly decide not to change and gradually (or sometimes rapidly) go out of business and become extinct.

Few would do this on purpose, but it's the unintended consequences of not changing that are the heart of the issue. Senior leaders who do a head-fake on themselves, thinking they're changing their behavior and imagining this change is what their employees see, feel, and believe, are in for a rude awakening. This disconnect between senior leaders and their employees is entirely real in companies, as confirmed by the Capgemini study, particularly with dysfunctional senior leadership behaviors present.

Look closely at your all-colleague survey scores, particularly any scores around employee engagement. Ask yourself if 80% of your employees coming to work happy is the best you can do. Is that acceptable? That number still means 20% aren't. That's one in five people. For a company of 500, you're saying it's okay for a hundred people to not be fully engaged.

If you're serious about transformational change, then this traditional benchmark KPI needs to see the inside of a trash bin.

There's no reason we can't create a future company environment where everyone is fully engaged.

I see doubters shaking their heads. But really, if you could imagine a workplace where everyone aligns around a few top goals, where radical ideas about change and disruption are openly discussed and embraced, and where fear is stamped out of the organization—wouldn't you want to work there?

I would.

In Table 2, I present my list of items where I have observed the gulf between the perspective of senior leaders and that of the employees. As noted, this is not an all-inclusive list, but each item is a critical element in the cultural health of the company. When a culture is unhealthy, these are the items that foster cynicism and mistrust, lead to employee turnover, and prevent companies from achieving transformational change. When your industry is being radically disrupted by new technologies, new business models, and new competitors, an unhealthy company acts frozen in time. It is unable to get off the tracks when it sees the freight train barreling toward it.

On the other hand, when the culture is healthy, these are the critical items that result in cross-functional alignment of goals, trust in senior leadership, retention of key employees, and an environment where you can address disruptive challenges.

Bridging this gap is the subject of the rest of this book.

In the EMPLOYEE column of Table 3, I have shown the employee perspective on these key items when senior leaders do in fact bridge the gap. It takes a transformational change within a company to make it happen and to make it stick. My own experience, confirmed by Capgemini in their recent study, suggests we have no choice but to tackle this transformational change. It all starts with the Service Revolution!

TABLE 2: The gap between senior leader and employee perspectives on key company culture points:

Senior Leaders Believe	Employees See and Feel
Stretch goals	Unrealistic expectations
Direct and blunt talk	Abrasive, condescending tone
Go fast, follow process	Chaos and lack of clarity
Focus on top priorities	Everything is a priority
Performance management	Time for blame and shame
Talent development	DIY/you're on your own
Active listening	Mind is already made up
Collaboration	Collaboration = do it my way!
Recognition	Boss never says thank-you*
Diverse opinions valued	Naysayers aren't team players
Management commitment	Leaders don't follow-through
Customers are number one	Just another slogan, flavor of the week
We value your opinion	Then why is the communication so poor?

* In a Wichita State University survey, employees rated a manager's thanks as THE MOST motivational incentive of all. Unfortunately, 58% of the employees said they rarely received a personal thank you. From the employees' points of view, their managers were takers. They took their employee's efforts but didn't give much recognition in return.

Remember, perception is reality! It doesn't matter how well-intentioned the senior leadership is or that they believe what they're doing will make a difference. In my experience, senior leaders drink their own bathwater and see things only as they want to see them.

It's what the employees perceive to be true that constitutes a company's existing reality. No company should accept such a divergent view between what senior leaders think and what employees believe. Senior leaders need to be less me-centered and more we-centered. Less self-absorbed in their own agenda. Less caring only about the business. And more focused on the company's employees and the critical transformational changes that will be required to survive and thrive as businesses and industries go through significant disruption.

When done right, as we'll see in the upcoming chapters, the perspectives of senior leaders AND employees become aligned, setting the stage for transformational changes to occur. Then the Service Revolution can start!

Table 3 reflects the same items in Table 2, showing the employee perspective that results when senior leaders are aligned and their dysfunctional behavior goes away.

TABLE 3: No gap between senior leader and employee perspectives on key company culture points:

Senior Leaders Believe	Employees See and Feel
Stretch goals	Challenging opportunities
Direct, blunt talk	You know where you stand
Go fast, follow process	Fast pace, never bored
Focus on top priorities	Clear alignment and expectations
Performance management	Good feedback, able to improve
Talent development	Good performers are valued
Active listening	Senior leaders hear me
Collaboration	Cross-functional alignment
Recognition	Feel appreciated
Diverse opinions valued	Okay to disagree
Management commitment	Trust in management
Customers are number one	Customer-centric mindset in all areas
We value your opinion	My contributions really matter

CHAPTER SEVEN TAKEAWAYS

- There is a gulf between what senior leaders think and believe and what employees see and feel.

- A Capgemini study dramatically illustrates the stark gap in beliefs between leaders and employees in several key areas. These include:

  - Innovation

  - Data-Driven Decision Making

  - Collaboration

  - Open Culture

  - Digital First Mindset

  - Agility and Flexibility

  - Customer-Centricity

- These gaps must be bridged for leaders and employees to become aligned, build trust, and together tackle the disruptive changes that will occur in their industry and company.

- This new alignment will create the energy and opportunity to launch a transformational change through a Service Revolution.

Part Two
PRACTICES

Chapter Eight

Key Steps to Jumpstart Your Service Revolution

"Wherever you see a successful business, someone once made a courageous decision."

PETER DRUCKER

L ike you, I've read a lot of books putting forward outstanding theories on how to make a company better. However, most begin and end with theory and never provide concrete examples of putting the theory into practice.

That unfinished ending leaves our heads packed with good ideas but no practical outlet. The ideas just rumble around and get connected to other ideas—many not relevant to the larger issue—and as a result, nothing happens. Or what does happen is far off the mark of what we intended with our original idea.

My goal in part two of this book is to walk through a real-life personal example that demonstrates the power of the seven key steps of the Service Revolution. As we progress, I will provide questions you can discuss with other leaders on your team or across your company.

Before we get to those key steps, let's pause for a moment and recall in simple terms what EXTERNAL customers and INTERNAL customers (employees!) want.

If our goal is to define and implement steps to create a service-centered, customer-centric culture, having the needs of external and internal customers top of mind seems more than reasonable.

What Do External Customers Want?

- Any issue resolved with a single phone call. Or no phone call at all. Or with one click online.

- Not having to repeat their story over and over as they deal with multiple agents or touch points. (My apologies if I triggered a flashback to your own bad experiences with the cable company.)

- Someone to take full ownership to resolve their issue.

What Do Internal Customers (Employees) Want?

- Consistent, clear, and continuous communication of information, particularly from management.

- True alignment of goals between departments where everyone works to achieve the same goal (they don't just say they're doing so).

- Less time spent on unproductive, inefficient work tasks.

A 2016 survey by McKinsey & Company found a clear correlation between a company's customer-centric thinking and employee satisfaction. Specifically, they determined that at the lowest level, if people were courteous, helpful, and available, then employees held a good opinion of the company as courteous and helpful. That's okay, but not a bell-ringing, retention-grabbing bar to reach for. At the highest level, when a company had a service-centered, customer-centric culture, employee satisfaction went way up, with employees enjoying a seamless experience within their company about any issue that needed solving. Moreover, the resolution typically occurred on the first pass.

What this shows is that the Service Revolution is good for your company on all fronts. It offers significant benefits not only for the happiness of your external customers but also for raising the engagement and satisfaction of your internal customers, your employees.

As we all know from our experience (and Patrick Lencioni), "Culture eats strategy for lunch." To be specific, unless companies create the winning culture needed to compete for customers as well as top talent employees, they can't fully succeed as their future unfolds. It's why we've touched again and again on the critical factor of employee engagement. And why I keep pointing out that employee engagement can be completely undone by senior leaders with institutional blindness and dysfunctional behaviors.

Finally, let me be clear on a couple of points. The Service Revolution isn't in lieu of whatever product and market strategies you have today or in place of the important metrics around sales revenue, profitability, and ROI. Rather, I'm proposing the ADDED company-wide effort to completely transform how INTERNAL company people, functions, and departments work in concert to create a NEW service-centered, customer-centric culture.

I honestly believe that companies don't have a choice. And—as stated above—it just makes good common sense. One final analogy to make this point.

Everyone who goes to a nice restaurant expects great food and great service. How do you feel if the food is great but the service lousy? Or what if food and service are both outstanding but you wait forever for your bill (perhaps because the person running the register didn't prioritize your bill)? Or maybe you asked to substitute asparagus for green beans, and the waitperson came back and said the kitchen didn't allow substitutions (another support person who could care less about accommodating changes). It's a simple example of how internal support people make a huge difference in the customer experience.

Now think of your own business. Try calling your own toll-free number as if you were the customer. How difficult is it to wade through the phone tree? Can you easily get past the auto-attendant and talk to a real person? And when you do, is that person courteous, knowledgeable, and driven to serve and resolve issues—or just make excuses?

My cable company provides an awful example. After giving the auto-attendant all the requested security information (address, phone number, social security number, super-secret pin number, shirt size, favorite ice cream flavor, etc.), a live person quizzes me on the same questions all over again. What a crazy time waste.

Or maybe your own call center's metric is low talk-time, so reps are incented to rush you off the phone. Be honest now. How does that feel?

Or how about your most pressing company issue? How are cross-collaboration issues delaying results? When do people tackle the key issues in assembly-line fashion—and sub-optimize the eventual resolution? What patterns do you see of blaming the project manager or various functional managers?

Or maybe the real issue runs much deeper: Your company doesn't have, understand, or live into a service-oriented, customer-centric culture. You need a culture where all the individuals, functions, and departments of the organization live into a new culture that is service-centered and customer-centric, where the sum of the parts makes harmonious music and not a bunch of raucous noise.

The Process in Practice: Real-World Example of Success

Here are the key steps that need to be taken. We'll cover each in some detail to ensure clarity. Granted, no two situations are alike, so there may be some variability in your implementation of the seven steps. I'm NOT saying you should make stuff up as you go along or get so far outside the guardrails that the step you're taking isn't recognizable. The seven steps are all critical. That said, I would rather see 90% execution of a step done with passion and commitment than 100% adherence while people are only going through the motions. The classic check-the-box process for implementation won't cut it when you embark on transformational change.

I'm talking real change management here, with everyone on board, especially senior leaders. With passion. With commitment. With energy. With clear understanding and acceptance that some tasks are difficult and may not be successful on the first effort. Learn from it and keep moving forward!

To simplify the discussion around implementation of the seven steps and then show a real example of successful execution, I have organized the seven steps around three key themes:

Theme #1: It all starts with senior management (Steps One, Two, and Three)

Step One
Commit to jumpstart the Service Revolution from the CEO and senior leadership on down, proving complete buy-in not just with words but with actions.

Step Two
Create a common vision of the Service Revolution, a compelling company change story that vividly describes your company's service-centered future state.

Step Three
Communicate your inspirational and aspirational company change story of the Service Revolution to every employee.

Theme #2: Leaders need followers and followers need to lead (Steps Four and Five)

Step Four

Identify specific work behaviors needed to create the Service Revolution across all INTERNAL functions and departments. Brainstorm and debate. Call out negative habits and codify specific positive expectations.

Step Five

Form cross-functional transformation teams with members from each internal function to map processes to achieving the new company change story and apply specific work behaviors of the Service Revolution.

Theme #3: Believe with your heart and soul and act with a sense of discovery, not fear. No bystanders! (Steps Six and Seven)

Step Six

Identify, prioritize, and publicize the new metrics that will measure and sustain the Service Revolution.

Step Seven

Stamp out fear and provide strong rewards and recognition for each achievement of the Service Revolution.

We will relive each of these key themes (and steps) through the lens of a real example I was privileged to lead.

CHAPTER EIGHT TAKEAWAYS

- Jumpstarting a Service Revolution inside your company is new ground to cover. And the change is transformational, not incremental.

- The Service Revolution is NOT a substitute for critical business metrics which are in place today, like revenue, profit, asset management, and customer loyalty.

  - The Service Revolution is instead a critical culture shift within the company that empowers it to address disruptive change.

  - It creates an engaged workforce that works together like an orchestra, crisply aligned, with no daylight around a few common goals.

- Customers want great service and accountable company employees. They expect issues to be resolved on first contact.

- Employees want challenging work that is critically aligned with company priorities, a leadership team that shoots straight, and the absence of the noise and chaos created by mis-aligned group priorities and cross-functional collaboration that exists in name only. (And how about spending some time and resources on my career development?)

- There are three key themes of the Service Revolution, which sum up the seven critical steps to achieve your Service Revolution.

CHAPTER NINE

It All Starts with Senior Management

(Steps One, Two, and Three)

*"The most exhausting thing in life,
I have discovered, is insincerity."*

ANNE MORROW

Step One
Commit to jumpstart the Service Revolution from the CEO and senior leadership on down, proving complete buy-in not just with words but with actions.

Step Two
Create a common vision of the Service Revolution, a compelling company change story that vividly describes your company's service-centered future state.

Step Three
Communicate your inspirational and aspirational company change story of the Service Revolution to every employee.

Our organization had arrived at a crossroads. The company had grown dramatically, organically as well as through acquisition. Our customers were satisfied with our products but not our service and support.

Part of this situation was self-inflicted though not intentional. Over the years we had acquired several companies and let them run autonomously. Not totally, but their organizational structures were like stand-alone companies, each with sales and service staff calling on the same customer base. These stand-alone product divisions served the exact same corporate customers!

The patience of our customers was wearing thin. Who were they supposed to call when they had a problem? Our products and solutions all worked in sync as a total system for our customers. When the system broke down, the cause could well be one of the diverse products and solutions sold by our various divisions. The customer had to isolate the issue on their own and attempt to identify its most likely cause.

Complicated stuff.

Guess what happened.

The customer called the division servicing the product they identified as the culprit, only to be told, "No, our product couldn't possibly be causing the problem. It must be a product from another division."

Pause for a moment. These customers had purchased several hundred thousand dollars of equipment and in many cases millions of dollars. If these products didn't work in harmony, the customer couldn't operate their facility and would lose sales. It was critical that problem resolution be instantaneous, cost-effective, and hassle-free.

It wasn't. When a major issue struck, each division sent their local sales person AND service person to the site to resolve the problem, meaning as many as ten salespeople and ten service people would arrive at the same customer to work on the same problem. We might as well have shown up in a fleet of clown cars. Or a clown bus.

Most troubling, the presence of all these people ignited a game of pass-the-buck, with everyone stepping through a process of elimination to prove it wasn't their product causing the breakdown. There was so much blame-avoidance going on that no one focused on fixing the problem and making the customer happy!

There had to be a better way. I was chartered by the CEO to figure out what it was and get it up and running.

I realized I needed help, so we engaged a consulting firm to assist. Together we solicited the perspectives of our CEO and division presidents on what we could do to more easily, quickly, and accurately resolve customer issues.

Service Revolution Step One

We were commencing Step One: "Commit to jumpstart the Service Revolution from the CEO and senior leadership on down, proving complete buy-in not just with words but with actions."

The consensus among senior leaders was that we needed to create a separate service and support division as the touchpoint for all customer service issues. That said, not everyone had the same vision for what that would look like, particularly how it would be organized and managed.

After weeks of fact-gathering and analysis, I presented the business plan to the senior leaders, including the CEO. The plan included merging all existing divisional field service people into one larger field service organization and creating a new call center where all customers could call for service. We also set up groups for HR, Finance, Marketing, Technical Support, Training, and Parts and Logistics within the new service organization to support the effort.

This new division wouldn't only be a one-stop-shop for our customers to obtain service. We also designed it as a profit center selling our services at a healthy margin. The service teams spread across several divisions had always been a cost center.

Admittedly, these were big changes. The division presidents had to surrender their field service teams to the new division.

This staff shift is still called "headcount" in many companies today. Not an endearing word for describing real live people. Can you imagine referring to your spouse and kids as "headcount"?

I didn't think so.

But despite initial angst and territorialism by some division presidents, the senior team recognized that the larger company needed to change how it conducted service. The need expressed by our customers was too compelling to ignore and maintain the status quo.

In a nutshell, the company put its money where its mouth was, allowing us to set up a new organization to better serve our customers. We had complete-buy in from all senior leaders.

Did buy-in come easily? No. Front-line service people had a strong allegiance to their respective divisions, and they felt unsettled when we transferred them to a new organization with different managers. The local sales people expressed dismay that "their" service person was now in a different group and worried their new service person might not be as responsive to customer problems.

Let me offer some additional detail on how you can implement Step One.

Implementing Step One

Commit to jumpstart the Service Revolution from the CEO and senior leadership on down, proving complete buy-in not just with words but with actions.

I know that senior level buy-in sounds like a cliché. I'm sure you've read dozens of books on leadership, management strategy, culture, and more that preach the need for C-level and senior leadership commitment and support.

So what? C-level support is always essential. The difference here is that I'm pressing you to demonstrate commitment through action, not just words.

In chapter four we covered the organizational trust problems that result when senior leaders say one thing and do another. Remember Lou Mahigel's advice: "Skip the words, watch the behaviors."

As we've seen from many examples, most senior leadership teams have an institutional blind spot here. They say the right things—sincerely, I hope—but the messages heard by employees seem disingenuous. The employees instinctively know that there is no way the pontifications of senior leaders will ever become a reality. Words are spoken. Trust is broken. And the results fall far short of the promises.

Consequently, for major cultural initiatives like a Service Revolution, the CEO and the senior leadership team need to be in lock-step IN THEIR BEHAVIORS. They need to constantly recall that employees are watching their behaviors and are keenly aware of any disconnects. *Is my department VP saying and doing the same things that the CEO is saying and doing?* People pick up on small and seemingly harmless signs that senior leaders aren't aligned. And this just reinforces common bad behaviors—working in silos, performing tasks unrelated to the company's top three initiatives, and thinking of the customer as something abstract, or not thinking about the customer at all.

Your company lives or dies on whether you jumpstart the Service Revolution. Your future success depends on it! So before going public with an initiative to transform the culture to be service-centered and customer-centric, it's critical that the C-level team have a clear picture of what they want and a complete, unified commitment to execute the initiative. They must demonstrate this commitment through consistent, positive behaviors visible to employees. It's the only way to build trust in the company so you can be successful.

Not easy at all. But unequivocally essential. To use a favorite old expression, "This dog won't hunt without it."

With senior leadership resoundingly committed to the new initiative, it's now time for Step Two, getting all employees to understand and be on board with the important changes that lie ahead

Service Revolution Step Two

At this point, Step Two became critical: "Create a common vision of the Service Revolution, a compelling company change story that vividly describes your company's service-centered future state."

Within the business plan—as well as in every communication with existing division employees—we kept repeating our new common vision:

- ONE phone number for ALL service calls.

- ONE service management system to track customer service history.

- ONE common set of service metrics.

- ONE happy customer!

With staunch support from senior management and a compelling vision for customer service, we created a future vision the customer enthusiastically embraced. Just as important, so did the people impacted by the change. It was hard to argue with the key elements of the new compelling vision:

- ONE CALL to the call center to initiate service was far more efficient and cost-effective than multiple call points.

- Dispatching the RIGHT SERVICE PERSON to the customer site was clearly better than sending up to 10 service people to shift responsibility for the customer's problem.

- Logging ALL CUSTOMER SERVICE ISSUES IN ONE SERVICE MANAGEMENT SYSTEM made information far more accessible than having pockets of customer information scattered across the company. It was especially helpful when we wanted to mine that data for more ways to improve customer service, add value, and differentiate ourselves from competitors. The result was higher revenue and profit from selling better service agreements.

- ONE SET OF METRICS ensuring consistent response times, first-time fix, and on-hand trunk stock for spare parts was far better than a smorgasbord of service performance metrics within the same company. How could we ever have thought it was okay for several service techs to go to a single site for the same problem with a different set of performance metrics?

It became obvious that delivering superior customer service to our customers was essential and far more important than maintaining our existing structure and service performance—which was expensive, random, and unsustainable—as customer expectations were rising.

Implementing Step Two

Create a common vision of the Service Revolution, a compelling company change story that vividly describes your company's service-centered future state.

With senior management completely onboard with the criticality of the new initiative to jumpstart a Service Revolution, you need a vision of what this future-state looks like, stated in simple terms all employees can understand.

This step is immensely harder than most people think. I can't count how many times I've been on the receiving end of messages about new initiatives, only to be—underwhelmed.

The senior leader making the pitch was usually speaking over the employees, not to them in a way that conveyed sincerity. Not only that, but key messages disappeared in far too many PowerPoint slides jammed with far too much technical detail.

I often looked around the room to see a crowd confused by what they were hearing. Worse yet, I could see the fog rolling in and eyes glazing over. People didn't get the point, nor did they have the courage to raise their hand and request a re-do. Time and again, an important opportunity was missed to energize the company around an exciting key initiative.

What could have happened instead?

You likely weren't around when then-President John F. Kennedy proclaimed this audacious vision: "I believe that this Nation should commit itself to achieving the goal, before this decade is out, of landing a man on the moon and returning him safely to earth."

Let those words sink in. Those words rang out more than half a century ago!

You can hear them for yourself by searching online for *John F. Kennedy "Landing a Man on the Moon" Address to Congress May 25, 1961.*

You can't help but notice the marvelous simplicity and directness in President Kennedy's choice of words. It didn't matter if you were a CEO, a waiter in a diner, an office assistant, a student, factory worker, or religious leader. You instantaneously grasped the vision. There was no lack of clarity, all captured in a couple of dozen words. Contrast that with dozens of PowerPoint slides and hours of management-speak!

President Kennedy's vision was all the more amazing because he spoke this call to action knowing the country lacked the technology to achieve the goal—for now. We didn't have rocket engines developed to launch a space vehicle, materials to enable the space capsule to withstand the heat of re-entry into the Earth's atmosphere. John Glenn hadn't yet orbited the Earth, so we didn't even have practical proof that human beings could break free of gravity and head to the moon.

Kennedy's vision galvanized the nation. He dreamed big. He painted an enticing picture of the future. And his words and many that followed imparted a clear understanding of the goal and what it would take to get there.

In Step Two, senior leaders must create a compelling story about what the company's future will look like once the Service Revolution has occurred. I submit that the task is much easier than what JFK and the country undertook in 1962. We have sophisticated tools and processes for measuring and improving customer satisfaction of existing EXTERNAL customers. We simply need to pivot to the inside and project what it would look like if every individual, function, and department in the company acted as if everyone else in the company was their INTERNAL customer.

People retain material presented in a vivid image. While there is no one right way to do this, there are plenty of wrong ways. The real test of your company story is whether it is:

- Compelling and vivid

- Immediately understood by everyone who hears it

- Short and easily repeatable

- Energizing for all

- A challenge to the prevailing conventional wisdom

- Continually spoken about by your CEO and senior leaders

Once you have your story, you're ready for Step Three.

Service Revolution Step Three

With senior management fully aligned and a new compelling vision for the future, we proceeded to build momentum
across the organization by communicating incessantly what
was changing and why.

**That's Service Revolution Step Three: "Communicate your
inspirational and aspirational company change story of
the Service Revolution to every employee."**

I would honestly say we over-communicated. But that's what
it takes. When making large strategic changes, people need to
hear, understand, and believe the message conveyed by senior
management. That takes repetition bordering on the obnoxious.

My story so far invites an obvious question. Given our severe
problem with providing Service Excellence to our customers,
shouldn't we have seen the problem sooner and done something
to fix it? Of course. But that wasn't our reality. Truthfully, we
can all look within our companies and see unresolved problems, underperforming groups, and unmet goals.

The key isn't to look in the rearview mirror and say, "How
come?" Better to look out the windshield and say, "Why not?"
Why not do something NOW and make life better for our customers and our company. After all, if we don't our customers
could leave us for the competition.

Understanding how critical this strategic change was to our
company, you can see why it was imperative to gain senior
leadership buy-in, create a compelling new vision for the future state, and communicate this new vision in an inspiring
way that motivates aspirational expectations.

These three vital steps marked the beginning of our Service Revolution. The irony is that our Service Revolution involved establishing a new service division. The Service Revolution in your company may be different. But in every case, the steps are the same.

Implementing Step Three

Communicate your inspirational and aspirational company change story of the Service Revolution to every employee.

Every employee in your organization must hear your inspirational, aspirational change story again and again. Which means your story must be communicated over and over and over—and then, over again.

Change management isn't a core competency of most companies I've observed. The teams I've been part of always struggled to get the message right, much less master how and when to communicate it. Frankly, we treated change more like an event than a journey. Management raced to assemble beaucoup PowerPoint slides, then stashed the message away until the next regular town hall or another company-wide meeting. The communication was delivered by senior leaders unpersuaded by the case for change and therefore lacking the power to spur adoption. People were well intended. They just didn't know how to give a moonshot speech.

The effort would come off half-baked, and employees predictably took a mindset of "Give it time, and this too shall pass." Hardly the energized curiosity and mobilization needed for aligned, collaborative action.

How do you know if your people have caught the story? Observe people. Do you sense urgency? Can you sense excitement about the future? Have people stopped holding back their discretionary time? Are they pressing you with questions about moving forward? Does it suddenly feel like your team is playing to win rather than simply trying not to lose? What's the buzz?

The answers to these questions will guide you as you communicate and recommunicate your change story.

When you communicate, keep it short, simple, and inspiring. Above all, be authentic. As you talk to employees about jumpstarting the Service Revolution, show up like it's your son or daughter's birthday party. Be excited. Anticipate fun.

It's more than fine to be aspirational. Your company may not be equipped to do everything it takes to complete your Service Revolution. Remember, President Kennedy declared we would land on the Moon before 1969 came and went knowing his call to action was aspirational, nothing short of OVER-THE-MOON. There were technology issues our country hadn't yet solved.

Being aspirational is energizing. It motivates most people. Conquering the unknown provides new opportunities, as long as the company environment embraces failure as one of the necessary steps on the way to success.

Communicating your change story should be a breakpoint moment for your company and senior leaders. You're declaring the future you want, a new world where employees don't just survive but thrive.

There will be distractions and hiccups in execution. That's life. But the resolve senior leaders model for all employees will enable the company to internalize this new way of doing business and alter the cultural DNA of the company.

When that happens—and you can see it—you'll know you're on the right track.

CHAPTER NINE TAKEAWAYS

- The CEO and Senior leadership MUST demonstrate through actions—not just words—their complete buy-in to jumpstarting the Service Revolution in the company.

- The Service Revolution requires a common vision, a compelling company change story that describes in simple, understandable words what your company's service-centered, customer-centric future looks like.

- This aspirational change story must be communicated over and over to everyone in the company with clarity and inspiration.

Implementation Discussion Questions for Steps One, Two, and Three

Answer these questions regarding jumpstarting the Service Revolution in your organization:

- Where is your company experiencing disruption—or where does it see it coming to your industry? How are disruptors winning business from your company?

- To what extent does senior management show genuine concern for disruption? What relevant actions do you see?

- Where does the effort to deal with disruption rank among company priorities? What is more important? When have you observed verbal commitments to change not backed up by action?

- How does senior management live out a commitment to creating a service-centered culture within your company? What dollars and people are dedicated to the effort?

- If senior leadership isn't creating a service-centered culture, what counterproductive behaviors do you observe?

- What compelling vision has senior management created for your company's future? Why is this vision compelling for you and others in the company?

- How do you rate the future vision for its ease of understanding, inspirational impact, and aspirational reach? What details do people buy into? How do you know?

CHAPTER TEN

Leaders Need Followers and Followers Need to Lead

(Steps Four and Five)

Step Four
Identify specific work behaviors needed to create the Service Revolution across all INTERNAL functions and departments. Brainstorm and debate. Call out negative habits and codify specific positive expectations.

Step Five
Form cross-functional transformation teams with members from each internal function to map processes to achieving the new company change story and apply specific work behaviors of the Service Revolution.

Committing to the cause, creating an inspiring new story, and communicating the vision is fun. It's your jumpstart to the Service Revolution. But I'll be honest. There's more heavy lifting if you want to succeed.

As our team began our Service Revolution, we sensed we had survived a critical foundational phase. Senior leadership supported our creation of a new service division bringing brand new functions. We began moving people from our existing divisions to the new service organization.

Consider the magnitude of that change. Would that redistribution of employees fly in your company? What resistance would you meet? Would leaders willingly surrender their people for the greater good?

Plenty of leaders think ME ahead of WE. They calculate their wins and losses in cold, impersonal terms, like who has the biggest headcount. They do their utmost to maintain the size and scope of their oversight. This reinforces why the Service Revolution is hard to do but essential to get done. We're breaking chains that keep us locked in today's reality. We need to show the way to a new tomorrow where senior leaders put WE before ME and treat people as people.

Let's get back to my real-world example.

Service Revolution Step Four

After our initial work on the new service division, we had tremendous forward momentum. But what came next? Sure, we could bring people onboard. But what did we want them to do? What did our unique situation require our employees to do differently?

We were ready for Step Four: "Identify specific work behaviors needed to create the Service Revolution across all INTERNAL functions and departments. Brainstorm and debate. Call out negative habits and codify specific positive expectations."

Thankfully, as we showed the way to a new future, we had a compelling new vision to guide us. If we were going to truly be a one-stop shop delivering memorable (superior) service, we had to define the behaviors we wanted to instill and reward.

We saw a huge need for new behaviors. An immediately obvious need arose as we integrated field service staff from existing product divisions. Their being dispatched by the new call center required completely new behaviors from them. After receiving the dispatch call, the service tech had a specific time frame to call the customer to set up an onsite appointment. Because a breakdown had halted the customer's operations, same-day service was almost always the rule. That said, we expected the service tech to juggle multiple critical calls.

Again, a new moment of truth. The customer anxiously awaited the tech's arrival to resolve the problem. But the fact that the tech had called and set the appointment—often with self-service tips to get the customer started—set an expectation that the field tech would arrive as promised. Contrast that with the previous system, where the customer hung up the phone and hoped help would show up—someday.

We also had new expectations around communication for internal technical support. Field service staff are resourceful, brutally honest, and incredibly loyal. But they don't know everything, even the 20-year veterans. Our expectation that technical support provide a nearly instant response to the field was another new behavior to instill and reward. What good does it do to have the most customer-friendly dispatch system if service techs get to the site and see a problem they can't fix?

Technical support couldn't go MIA. We were all for vacation days and long lunches, but we also needed to ensure we were living into our new vision of delivering superior customer service. The technical support team found a way to juggle work hours and personal commitments to serve the field service techs who were serving the end customer.

When I say Step Four involves identifying necessary behaviors across all internal functions, that includes management.

Along our journey to the Service Revolution, we had to call out negative leadership behaviors. This step might be the toughest of all for most companies. Institutional blind spots make this highly difficult.

For example, most organizations have company values statements, written cultural norms, and policies on how they expect people to show up. Most organizations claim to have an open communication policy where employees can step forward and speak up.

When they do, management promptly shoots the messenger.

The manager doing the shooting doesn't see it that way. They perceive themselves as capable leaders providing direct feedback around an employee's flawed point of view. In their own eyes, they've just done a good deed.

You can bet the employee will bury their next suggestion or new product idea.

As will anyone else privy to the exchange. The result is a company with fear stamped into its psyche, where conflict avoidance becomes the norm. Management will remain oblivious to the real problem. They just won't see it.

Next-of-kin to these institutional blind spots is another big problem, but the behavior is much more pernicious. Senior leaders insert themselves and try to control the process.

Here are a few real examples we encountered with senior leaders:

- Hijacking a team meeting by continually providing their opinion about what should be happening. **Translation:** "Why aren't you doing things my way?"

- Texting or doing email when you're presenting an important topic. **Translation:** "What you're saying isn't important. YOU aren't very important."

- Displaying negative body language—crossed arms, shaking heads, rolling eyes, gestures and sighs that indicate disinterest, dislike, or dis–something! **Translation:** "I'm important, maybe even arrogant—but I'm the boss."

- Telling employees how great things are—and that we're making good progress on our objectives. Followed by talk of cost-cutting and downsizing in a closed meeting later that day. **Translation:** "I'm allowed to say one thing and do another, even at the cost of employee trust."

Calling out these institutional blind spots and controlling behaviors of senior leaders is essential to drive culture change. But how?

Implementing Step Four

Identify specific work behaviors needed to create the Service Revolution across all INTERNAL functions and departments. Brainstorm and debate. Call out negative habits and codify specific positive expectations.

Clarifying behaviors necessary to the Service Revolution doesn't happen apart from an amazingly simple and astonishingly effective task. Write them down. In plain language.

This is a team sport, because the goal is to identify and document critical new behaviors that everyone will abide by, CEO and senior leadership included, to establish a pervasive culture of Service Excellence.

NO EXCEPTIONS.

Part of this effort must include explicit permission for employees to call out coworkers not living into agreed-to new behaviors. The call-out isn't personal. The receiver needs to receive the critique without becoming defensive. And senior leaders don't get a pass. All of this has to happen in a safe environment, a fear-free zone where people can point out behaviors with no recriminations, perceived or real.

While this process can help restore an otherwise unhealthy company culture, I'm specifically focused here on the day-in-day-out behaviors essential for the Service Revolution to change the DNA at the innermost core of a company.

The simple act of writing these new behaviors and expectations is powerful. Collaborating with large teams, or sub-teams with everyone involved, makes it even more powerful.

Once you've recorded these behaviors, post them. You could even paper over the old values as a physical reminder the change is real. This company is re-thinking how it functions internally. This company is changing for the better.

I've said there is no downside to great customer service. Likewise, there is no downside to creating a culture where fear is stamped out and new behaviors focused on Service Excellence become the norm.

Employees will be happier, engagement will be higher, trust will be stronger, tasks will get done faster, creativity and innovation will flourish, obstructions will fall, and your customers will experience dramatically better service.

What's wrong with this picture? Nothing!

Service Revolution Step Five

Back to our service division roll-out.

Our goal was to align the behaviors of all internal functions around delivering superior customer service to EXTERNAL and INTERNAL customers. With that key premise in mind, our cross-functional teams mapped new or improved processes for better serving the customer and each other.

That's Step Five: "Form cross-functional transformation teams with members from each internal function to map processes to achieving the new company change story and apply specific work behaviors of the Service Revolution."

Our all-new division management team stepped in and did outstanding work. I recruited from across the company, posting jobs and seeking out managers I believed would be best at creating and leading this new service division. I looked for leaders who liked new challenges, enjoyed working with each other, and most important, would give unfiltered feedback.

This new service management team became our first cross-functional transformation team. Together we set up new structures, hired people into our groups, and replicated additional cross-functional transformation teams. After all, we needed each other to create a new future. None of us knew all the right questions, much less the answers. But together we worked, laughed, struggled, and challenged each other to do the right thing.

And we got our service division off the ground with leading-edge processes. For example, in our new call center and technical support structure, we installed the most advanced service management system available. When a customer called for service, a page with that customer's name and complete call history opened on the call center agent's screen. After greeting the caller personally, the call center agent could immediately interact with the customer regarding their last service incident, with immediate access to the malfunctioning product, the resolution, and parts used in the repair. We could even see how the customer scored us on their last satisfaction survey.

And this was 30 years ago.

Nothing like this existed in our industry. We leaped ahead of our competitors. Soon it was obvious we could indeed differentiate ourselves by delivering superior customer service.

Were these changes easy? No.

Did we struggle not to fall back into old ways? Absolutely.

But we all felt this juice was worth the squeeze. To a person, everyone was committed, aligned, and dedicated to simplifying our processes and ensuring the most seamless service possible for customers outside and inside the company.

It's like when people say please and thank you. Or don't interrupt. Or hear you out before conjuring up a response. Or treat you with kindness even when no one is watching. Or offer help and guidance instead of caustic critique and blame.

These things aren't hard. We just make them hard. When a team collaborates to smooth out even the tiniest of bumps— even when you're driving in the dark—you can go places.

Implementing Step Five

Form cross-functional transformation teams with members from each internal function to map processes to achieving the new company change story and apply specific work behaviors of the Service Revolution.

The first four steps of the Service Revolution are about essential planning. To review:

- Step One: CEO and senior leadership commit to the change.

- Step Two: Create a common vision, an aspirational change story.

- Step Three: Communicate the change story loudly and repeatedly.

- Step Four: Brainstorm and record change management behaviors.

Step Five is about execution:

- Step Five: Form cross-functional teams to lay the track for the new culture train coming to town!

This new process roadmap varies by company. After all, every organization starts from a unique cultural baseline. Ironically, the more dysfunctional the company culture, the more energized people are to change it, assuming the company has solidly executed Steps One through Four. Companies with relatively subtle dysfunctional behaviors can face a greater challenge laying down new patterns critical to success because senior leaders can more easily slide back into previous behaviors unseen. Transformational champions will have to keep a sharp eye out for this and call out unhelpful behavior when they see it.

With that caution in mind, I believe the best way to start this roadmap for cross-functional transformation is to ask a lot of questions. Some suggestions:

- What subtle (and not so subtle) leadership behaviors need to radically change for the better?

- What could I do differently to serve my internal customer better? What measurable outcomes would ensure I deliver excellent service?

- What current behaviors could my functional peers change that will make my job more efficient and enjoyable? What new processes would break down roadblocks and achieve faster results?

- What behaviors exist across other functions that detract from the company's ability to increase customer satisfaction for external customers—and for internal customers?

- How can we help all internal support functions see their work as a direct contribution to improving customer satisfaction?

- Where do my behaviors fall short of Service Excellence? What new behaviors would meet that goal?

- What could internal support functions do differently to give front-line employees everything they need to create a WOW FACTOR for the customer?

- What are the "critical musts" vs. the "nice to haves" behaviors to achieve Service Excellence?

- Who isn't on board with changes necessary to achieve a Service Revolution? How can we get them on board? What needs to happen if they don't join in?

- How can we get this new roadmap in place and start living into new expectations and behavior norms?

- How do we keep going when these changes feel impossible to accomplish?

This list is just a start. But answering these questions will empower your cross-functional teams to readily identify and address any and all behaviors that get in the way of establishing a culture of Service Excellence within the company.

The real anti-roadblock test is this:

Does every business behavior and functional workstream move us toward our new future of sustainable Service Excellence?

If the answer is NO at any point, you're not reaching high enough. The changes you're undertaking aren't significant enough to achieve transformative change.

This is a pivotal moment where the CEO and senior leadership can make a huge positive impact. Their involvement on core teams—as participants, not leaders—inject much-needed encouragement, acceptance, recognition, and trust. When cross-functional teams see the senior team as true partners in change, the old boss/employee framework dissolves into authentic alignment and collaboration.

The beginning of the end for old ways and toxic behaviors will give rise to a new esprit de corps where the new partnership between senior leaders and employees across all functions and departments can powerfully remake the company culture.

Keep in mind this new culture is incredibly fragile at this point of the process. Senior leaders in particular must be watchful to ensure they don't slip back into bad behaviors. Leadership mess-ups—even if unintentional—can tank a culture change movement in a moment, taking long-term employee trust with it.

Conversely, employees need to practice—repeatedly—the new work patterns of a Service Excellence culture. They need to guard against old cross-functional battles, conflicting signals, misalignments, and other behaviors that don't support the customer. Patterns once tolerated must be called out and stamped out!

I can promise that people who have reached this point together will be working hard to make this movement a success.

It just feels right.

Common sense tells them that delivering top customer service to end customers is essential to customer loyalty. Why wouldn't a culture of Service Excellence within and across the company be just as important for employee loyalty?

CHAPTER TEN TAKEAWAYS

- Identifying necessary new behaviors is the next step in creating a Service Excellence experience across all internal functions and departments throughout the company.

- The simple act of writing down change management behaviors is a powerful motivation to change.

- Cross-functional transformation teams drawing members from each internal function must map processes that will achieve the change story.

- The CEO and the senior team should embed themselves as participants in transformation teams to demonstrate their ongoing support for change.

Implemention Discussion Questions for Steps Four and Five

Answer these questions regarding jumpstarting the Service Revolution in your organization:

- What percentage of people in your company can name the top three priorities in your company—can you? What is your proof? How has senior management provided crisp, clear, and consistent direction—or not?

- Do group leaders willingly share information and provide resources to support the company's top goals? What examples can you cite?

- Where do you see territorialism and too-heavy focus on departmental initiatives? What specific examples do you observe?

- How well do people from different groups work together on cross-functional teams to achieve company goals? What are some recent examples? How do you see trust tested and demonstrated among team members?

- What mechanisms do you have in place for calling out negative or dysfunctional behaviors by team members? What repercussions do you see for the person doing the behavior? For the person who points it out? When do you see this done positively? Negatively?

- How do you see people and teams acting like they're serving a customer, external or internal? Give examples of specific behaviors that demonstrate alignment of cross-functional teams in support of the end customer?

- How often do you talk about end customers in your work meetings? How do you bring the needs of the customer into your every-day work efforts, individually and as teams?

- When has the company undertaken a truly transformational change? What accomplishments resulted? How did cross-functional transformation teams drive the change? What were the results—positive or negative?

- How are you and your peers held accountable for achieving company changes necessary to compete in the future? How urgent are your efforts?

CHAPTER ELEVEN

Believe with Your Heart and Soul and Act with a Sense of Discovery, Not Fear. No Bystanders!

(Steps Six and Seven)

Step Six
Identify, prioritize, and publicize the new metrics that will measure and sustain the Service Revolution.

Step Seven
Stamp out fear and provide strong rewards and recognition for each achievement of the Service Revolution.

D espite occasional set-backs—some predictable, some not—our division management team and employees remained determined to succeed. When a challenge threw itself in front of us, we attacked head on!

Senior management had continued to support our Service Revolution. If anything, their backing had grown stronger, reinforcing our belief that we were on track. As we readied the public launch of our service center, our feelings of excitement and anticipation were almost boundless.

And then that first day came.

We were all huddled around our call center phones after weeks of announcing to customers our cut-over date—the day they should start calling our new 800 number for service. We wondered what the very first call would be. Which customer? Which product? Heck—would this all work as planned?

Minutes felt like hours, and the phone finally rang. Our first call came from a Florida customer who needed service on one of our products—ASAP.

The system worked. We were a happy team!

But let's back up and recount what happened before that first call.

Service Revolution Step Six

The whole purpose of the new division was to deliver superior customer service to our customers. To accomplish that we knew we had to decide and declare NEW METRICS for each team member.

That's Step Six: "Identify, prioritize, and publicize the new metrics that will measure and sustain the Service Revolution."

Metrics for the new call center were relatively easy. The service management system time-stamped everything, and our automatic call distribution switch tracked the wait time, when people hung up rather than wait any longer, and the duration of each customer interaction. We used this data to finetune the optimum number of agents, what additional training they needed, and what metrics would motivate them.

For people in field service, we focused on performance metrics such as:

- Time between call-center dispatch and a local field tech calling to set a service appointment.

- Time to arrive on site.

- Time to resolve the problem.

- First-time fix.

We also began sending customer satisfaction surveys. We found it crucial not just to post our performance to these metrics for all to see but to constantly invite team members to find ways to improve them.

We aimed to measure the right things and use the data to get better—and most likely faster. It's amazing how many firms get this backward. They measure the wrong things and then use the data they collect to beat up their people. When bosses use data as anything other than a learning tool, it's no surprise when employee engagement crashes.

At one company where I worked, the call center reported to a manager in a distant part of the company. His metric for agents was talk time. Not bad, but not entirely correct. Think about it. If you were a call center agent measured solely on talk time, with the goal of keeping customer encounters as short as possible, how would you behave?

You would seem rushed. You would engage with the customer as little as possible. You might even give less-than-complete answers to get off the phone. All the boss would see is that you handle calls quickly. He would walk by your cube and give you a high-five as you hang up the phone.

Call time? Under five minutes. Success? Not really.

The customer who called maybe just crashed a piece of equipment costing hundreds of thousands of dollars. They might feel panic. Or raging anger. Or they might accept a breakdown as a routine part of business that just needs to get dealt with. Whatever their mood, they want to call the service company and hear the soothing tones of a competent human being on the other end of the phone. They might need the agent to say everything will be okay. They might need to vent. They might even need some small talk about the weather or the latest sports score before describing their problem and arriving at a good resolution.

In our case of talk-time metrics, all they heard was a call center agent furiously typing minimal information followed by a snappy promise of a call from a local field service tech.

Click. Call ended. Field tech dispatched. Problem solved.

Until you look at the data.

It turned out that in any given year between one-quarter and one-third of all calls could be handled by the agent or with a quick check with another department WHILE THE CUS-TOMER WAS ON THE LINE.

If you do the math on 500,000 calls per year, that's over 150,000 calls a year that could have been resolved WITHOUT DISPATCHING A SERVICE TECH. The customer gets faster service, with enormous savings from not rolling a truck to a customer site.

As you implement your Service Revolution, make sure you get the right metrics and use the data for real improvement. And don't use data to beat up your front-line company representatives. Not good. For anyone.

Implementing Step Six

Identify, prioritize, and publicize the new metrics that will measure and sustain the Service Revolution.

We all know you can't improve something or gauge incremental progress against a goal unless you can measure it. It's best summed up in the adage "What gets measured gets done." I think this saying was coined by management guru Peter Drucker back in the 1960s, but other writers like Tom Peters and W. Edwards Deming also used it.

This reality is a conundrum for businesses. Almost all measures are lagging indicators of past performance, meaning we look in the rear-view mirror to see if we are still driving forward. These lagging indicators include:

- Company revenues

- Company profits

- Return on Investment (ROI)

- All-employee surveys

There's nothing wrong with these indicators, lagging or not. They're foundational to judging company performance. And individual outcomes. And determining compensation.

I don't see this changing anytime soon. We need solid financial metrics consistent from company to company to measure company performance against an industry. Investors want to gauge results relative to company peers. How else can they distinguish between a darling or a dog?

But lagging indicators are poor measures for transformational change. I've concluded that it's one reason transformational change takes so long—three or more years for many companies—and often fails. Following Drucker's logic, since we don't have good measures for transformational change, is it any wonder that it doesn't get done?

Most companies twist existing lagging indicators to make them a proxy for measuring progress on important future events, like transformational change. For example, if a company was outsourcing its manufacturing, it would predict future payments to the third-party company vs. the costs of retaining production. They look ahead to see if the ROI makes sense.

The company essentially takes incurred costs (a lagging measure) and projects future costs that will be incurred by outsourcing manufacturing (a quasi-leading indicator). I say "quasi" because it's a prediction of future costs, not a true metric of actual future costs.

That's relatively simple. But what if we wanted to measure our potential success of a transformational change to embed a service-centered, customer-centric culture throughout the company?

That's not so easy! Traditional employee engagement surveys can help, but they only measure employee perception at a specific point in time. They say nothing about context or concrete results. If a company has a bad quarter and stomachs are churning over the traditional lagging indicators of revenue and profitability, an employee engagement survey could flag the transformation as a failure—when in fact management is doing all the right things and making good progress on its transformational journey.

The solution is to identify, prioritize, and implement an entirely new set of metrics by which the service transformation will be measured and sustained. Keep in mind that this is unchartered territory. Most companies don't do this, and again, I believe it's one reason many transformation efforts fail.

So what metrics could we put in place? I would suggest the following starting points:

Map the end-to-end customer journey and hunt down disconnects. No matter the job or function, trace the work—in IT or

Engineering, for example—and map it as to how it eventually impacts the customer.

For example, if you're implementing a new order entry system to resolve a product ordering problem, how are actions measured from the perspective of the customer? Like how fast is the work getting done? How often does work get done right the first time? What delays are injected into the system by other functional groups, such as Quality or Marketing?

Being purposeful and honest with the facts shows how much work happens without a clear vision of its impact on the customer. It also exposes organizational tolerance for functional disconnects, work priorities not truly aligned, and/or people and functions operating on different timelines.

Prepare to be amazed by what you learn. Processes you thought were simple, straightforward, aligned across functions, and in sync with customer expectations often turn out to be just the opposite.

Send weekly internal communications highlighting what individual employees are doing to walk the talk on your company's inspirational change story. Include stories from senior leaders as well as individual contributors.

Of course, this presumes employees have come to understand Service Excellence and have bought into the transformational change story. If your previous communications haven't rung that bell, this will be an awkward exercise. It's tough for people to explain how their activities are helping build a service-centered, customer-centric culture when they haven't a clue what Service Excellence means for their role or how they are serving internal and external customers.

The good news is that these weekly personal testimonies from everyday employees have a huge net positive impact on the larger change story. They re-enforce that the company is, in fact, making progress on its transformational journey. And it's easy to measure. You either had a weekly story or you didn't.

Measure something entirely different that supports the transformation. You could start measuring the number of new ideas employees generate to help them better collaborate with their peers across functions. Note any proposals that would eliminate non-productive work and accelerate results. Then take the next step and track how many ideas are implemented. Companies preach this kind of thing but rarely measure the outcomes. I can hear Peter Drucker again, saying, "What gets measured, gets done."

Add customer-driven metrics. Most companies have metrics around a customer satisfaction rating, such as a Net Promoter Score (NPS), but these readouts are at best done monthly, and most often quarterly or even annually. The service transformation requires something simpler and more real-time.

Why not create mini-user groups of customers who will give you honest feedback—good or bad? You'll want several rotating groups to combat customer fatigue with the constant surveys they get from vendors. Your groups need to be simple, focusing on a couple of key items each time. I suggest a conference call or better yet, a video chat call where everyone can see each other. Calls should run from 30 to 60 minutes. Max. Alert these groups that your company is on a transformational mission to be service-centered and customer-centric. Ask them to be your eyes, ears, and conscience—your reality therapist.

If you welcome feedback in an open, non-defensive manner, customers will point out where you've let them down and what they expect from you going forward.

Ground rules? This user group isn't a bitch session. It isn't an occasion to resolve today's order entry problem. It's not an informal conversation that meanders on a course of its own. It's structured. There are couple points on which you want feedback.

Your role? JUST LISTEN. Let me repeat that. JUST LISTEN!

Customer discussions die when employees—particularly senior leaders—take over. They dive in to aggressively clarify. They argue, dispute, or rationalize what the customer is saying. Recall what happens when you do this to your employees. They either clam up or tell you what you want to hear, making your exercise in listening worthless.

I once conducted a conference call for key accounts of a company in complete denial about how customers viewed them. I invited all the senior leaders to participate, including the CEO. I knew which leader could be the problem child, but rather than single anyone out, I told the senior team—I didn't ask—that I was facilitating the questions and answers and that they were to LISTEN ONLY.

I selected six key customers to participate and sent ahead the questions I wanted to discuss. I added a few open-ended questions where the customer could say whatever was on their mind.

The call lasted exactly 60 minutes, and each of the six customers spoke. I only had to lunge for the mute button a couple of times as one senior leader grew agitated by the customers' reports.

After we hung up, the leaders sat stunned and silent. A few got defensive about the answers—or worse—that these were just "bad customers." (Really? Wow!) Over time, however, the leadership brought about significant change. Customers later reported they saw a real difference.

Commit to conducting these calls at least every other week. They aren't a real-time proxy for your NPS score. It's not a chance to test the latest new product concepts. You're simply asking for unfiltered feedback. It's a recurring report card from the customer viewpoint on how you're doing on the transformative journey.

As you wrap up, say "Thanks!" and "I look forward to speaking again soon!" And mean it. If you bring your customers into your transformation journey, inviting their unfiltered feedback, they will tell you exactly what you need to know.

Service Revolution Step Seven

This brings us to Step Seven: "Stamp out fear and provide strong rewards and recognition for each achievement of the Service Revolution."

Let me tell you how my real-world example turned out.

We did successfully launch the new service division. It was wildly successful and grew to be a multi-million-dollar organization generating above-average profitability. Each year a leading industry journal surveyed best products and best service.

The service division we created—our Service Revolution within the company—received top honors for delivering the best customer service in our industry! And we won that award for five years in a row!

By all measures, we were amazingly successful. Happy customers. Incremental revenue and profit for the company.

But my sweetest takeaway wasn't that. It was the exhilarating joy of working as a team, trusting each other and facing each issue with collaboration and alignment, achieving what we set out to do.

That teamwork was contagious. Top management continued to give us complete support even when things didn't go right. Instead of blame and shame, there was a helping hand to pull us forward. And we began including service people in the annual sales celebration, renaming the evening the Sales and Service Awards banquet. Winners brought their spouse or significant other to the event. We initiated a new tradition of giving Service Excellence awards to top field service techs. Service winners were chosen by the sales and account management teams. Imagine our satisfaction seeing salespeople argue why "their" service tech was the best!

The Seven Steps worked. Any fear of failure had been wiped out by a widespread commitment to a new future. All it took was a committed senior team, a compelling vision, and an aligned team that stuck together no matter what.

Implementing Step Seven

Stamp out fear and provide strong rewards and recognition for each achievement of the Service Revolution.

Transformational change is no time for incompetent leaders. When an organization incubates big change, the last thing you need is a crazy manager who runs around screaming, barking out orders. Seem far-fetched? Nope. I've seen way too many examples of leaders who "stamp in fear" rather than "stamp out fear."

The Service Revolution inevitably sputters and dies when employees have to spend their days doing mental combat with their peers or finding ways to stay below the bushes so their crazy boss doesn't yell at them.

When employees spend their time on defense within their organization, there's virtually no time and energy to go on offense, creating and implementing changes necessary to survive as an organization or even as individuals. And don't expect a Service Revolution! Who has time? Everyone is busy not getting things done, not collaborating, and not having fun.

Senior leaders must constantly walk the talk of the Service Revolution and ensure that organizational dynamics encourage change to start and spread. It's making Step Seven a never-ending Groundhog Day, giving the company's teams unconditional support to embrace change.

When this happens, and you make it through all seven steps, you're about to see something phenomenally rare in the workplace.

When employees don't have to work in fear, they have courage and capacity to embark on needed changes, even though most people are naturally change-resistant. Why? Because most people see change and take cover. They do everything possible to hide from anything that resembles a threat, because their dysfunctional leaders have promoted a dysfunctional culture of fear. Unfortunately, like all the companies highlighted in Chapter One, their organization will likely get hit by disruption. Market share will tank. Layoffs and budget cuts will follow. Senior leaders will make increasingly desperate and risky moves.

The Service Revolution will fail, and the march to extinction will continue unless we stop it right here.

At this point, I want to say, "C'mon, people. Let's get this right!"

Step Seven, in theory, should be the easiest to comprehend and put into practice. I mean—who wants to live in fear? And who doesn't like to be recognized for what they're doing? And rewarded—even if it's just a heartfelt thank you from your boss?

My observations show that most companies stumble here. It happens when companies are just doing their normal day-to-day. Now toss in the fact that the company has embarked on a transformational change, and you can understand why this step can be tough to pull off.

Let's spend a minute on "stamping out fear," a key point (number eight) in W. Edwards Deming's famous "14 Points for Management." They are part of his book *Out of the Crisis*, published decades ago in 1982.

Deming achieved fame by bringing his expertise around Total Quality Management to Japan, helping the country rebuild after WWII. His concepts gave birth to a manufacturing sector in Japan that became known for delivering high-quality products at affordable prices. Of course, I'm talking about Toyota. We all know how they brought GM and the Big 3 automakers to their knees by gobbling up automobile market share.

Deming gained his fame in Japan before the United States because domestic manufacturers didn't understand the value of his principles and process. They deemed him a fringe player—great theory, but not real in practice. He proved them wrong. (Later in life, mind you, Deming did play a leading role in Ford's reinvention with the launch and success of the Ford Taurus.)

So, what are Deming's 14 points and why are they important to us now? Read them for yourself and then I'll tell you what I think, remembering these were written long before most of today's employees even entered the workforce.

Dr. Deming's
14 Points for Management

1. **Create constancy of purpose** toward improvement of product and service, with the aim to become competitive and to stay in business, and to provide jobs.

2. **Adopt the new philosophy.** We are in a new economic age. Western management must awaken to

the challenge, must learn their responsibilities, and take on leadership for change.

3. Cease dependence on inspection to achieve quality. Eliminate the need for inspection on a mass basis by building quality into the product in the first place.

4. End the practice of awarding business on the basis of price tag. Instead, minimize total cost. Move toward a single supplier for any one item, on a long-term relationship of loyalty and trust.

5. Improve constantly and forever the system of production and service, to improve quality and productivity, and thus constantly decrease costs.

6. Institute training on the job.

7. Institute leadership. The aim of supervision should be to help people and machines and gadgets to do a better job. Supervision of management is in need of an overhaul, as well as supervision of production workers.

8. Drive out fear, so that everyone may work effectively for the company.

9. Break down barriers between departments. People in research, design, sales, and production must work as a team, to foresee problems of production and in use that may be encountered with the product or service.

10. Eliminate slogans, exhortations, and targets for the work force asking for zero defects and new levels of productivity. Such exhortations only create adversarial relationships, as the bulk of the causes of low quality and low productivity belong to the system and thus lie beyond the power of the workforce.

- Eliminate work standards (quotas) on the factory floor. Substitute leadership.

- Eliminate management by objective. Eliminate management by numbers, numerical goals. Substitute leadership.

11. **Remove barriers that rob the hourly worker of his right to pride of workmanship.** The responsibility of supervisors must be changed from sheer numbers to quality.

12. **Remove barriers that rob people in management and in Engineering of their right to pride of workmanship.** This means, inter alia, abolishment of the annual or merit rating and of management by objective.

13. **Institute a vigorous program of education and self-improvement.**

14. **Put everybody in the company to work to accomplish the transformation. The transformation is everybody's job.**[11]

If you didn't read those points twice, do it again and let them sink in.

---

11 Dr. Deming's 14 Points for Management, The W. Edwards Deming Institute, https://deming.org/explore/fourteen-points.

I think you'll arrive at the same conclusion I have, that these points remain as vibrant and valid today as they were decades ago when Deming wrote them. Point Number Eight—driving out fear so everyone can work effectively for the company— is the last step necessary to the Service Revolution, yet few follow it.

Obviously, there is still reason for fear in the workplace. Bad things happen to great people in good companies. Unfortunately, downsizes and restructures can happen anywhere, even in a healthy economy. Most people live with some existential fear of losing their jobs, and that fear does hurt morale and employee engagement.

But I don't think Deming was naïve on this point. I believe that "Drive out Fear" statement is pointed straight at managers and leaders. The dysfunctional behaviors of senior leaders create this very fear that Deming said we need to drive out, and the three most egregious behaviors I've pointed out surely top the list.

I'm sure Deming had other ideas about what leaders should do to drive out fear, but I doubt he would argue with the ones I've seen creating havoc inside organizations.

So the first critical message in Step Seven for jumpstarting your Service Revolution is to drive out fear, recognizing the dysfunctional behaviors described in this book and doing what is right.

The second part of Step Seven is to provide strong rewards and recognition at each step of the transformational journey. Companies and leaders will enjoy enormous gains of every kind if they recognize and reward people on the forefront of transformational change. So celebrate the effort your team is making. Small victories lead to winning battles. Simply saying thank you is one of the least used yet most powerful recognition tools you have.

At the end of Deming's treatise stands the most important point of all, the one that has dominated this book. Point 14 reads, "Put everybody in the company to work to accomplish the transformation. The transformation is everybody's job." Everybody in the company needs to be involved in the transformation, and transformation is everyone's job.

CHAPTER ELEVEN TAKEAWAYS

- Identifying and prioritizing new metrics allows the service transformation to be measured and sustained.

- Collaboration around metrics is essential between senior leaders and the cross-functional transformation team. The CEO must be completely onboard with these metrics.

- Stamping out fear and providing strong rewards and recognition during each step of the transformation journey keeps the Service Revolution alive.

- Deming foresaw that transformation of the company is essential and that it's everyone's job to be a part of it.

Implementation Discussion Questions For Steps Six And Seven

Answer these questions regarding jumpstarting the Service Revolution in your organization:

- How has senior management effectively articulated the Service Revolution—or not? What clear examples do you observe showing specific behaviors, actions, and results of management action?

- What clear, understandable, and achievable metrics have you put in place to measure your progress? How do they measure progress toward achieving your transformation? Who is on board—and how do you know?

- How is the Service Revolution being communicated across the company? How often do you hear about it? Do people believe? Give examples of specific communications by senior leadership and how these cascade to the entire organization.

- How is everyone—senior management especially— creating a culture of trust and recognition? Where do you experience fear and retribution? Why is this happening?

- How are people rewarded and recognized for their contributions toward achieving the Service Revolution? How frequently? Do people feel valued—or not? If people don't feel valued, what could you do to change that?

- What changes do your customers see in how your company provides products and services? Provide specific customer feedback on your company's transformation. What areas have improved the most? Which still need work?

- How well have employees internalized the belief that you're either serving the customer directly or serving someone who is? Give specific examples of this behavior being carried out. What departments or functions could better align in support of end customers?

Final Charge

Each person in a company needs to understand the PRI-ORITIES of the Service Revolution. What is the new future we're trying to create? But understanding WHAT matters and WHY isn't enough. We must all embrace the PRACTICES of living into a future where we serve customers both EXTERNAL and INTERNAL. How will we put all of this into action?

In the end, transformational change—results in the real world—is the measure our efforts. The Service Revolution should radically change what each of us does and how we do it. It was service guru and author Karl Albrecht who said, "If you aren't serving the customer directly, you better be serving someone who is."

Albrecht noted that within any organization, the more distant an employee is from serving the customer—or serving someone who is serving the customer—the more rigorously the organization must evaluate the necessity of that job. After all, with no visible connection to anything a customer values, how does the role matter to delivering superior customer service? And why would the customer be willing to pay for that job, given that the costs are ultimately passed along in the price paid for goods and services?

That concept has stuck with me my whole life. It's at the core of my thinking about the Service Revolution. Our work should add value to the external customer. If we can't connect the dots—perhaps a lot of dots—between our role and the end customer, then we need to reexamine how we spend our working hours.

And that brings me to my final charge to you. If the Service Revolution is the only way to fundamentally alter our corporate DNA and move toward a new future—and this transformational change is everyone's job (thanks, Dr. Deming!)—then you can't just wait for it to happen. **Your next step is obvious. Change doesn't begin with your coworkers. It begins with you.**

So what will you do TODAY to better serve your external customers? Or what will you do to better serve those internal customers who serve the end customer directly?

Your future depends on it!

Acknowledgments

Iremember when we had our first child. My wife, Kathy, did all of the hard work. I was there to ensure she breathed properly with each contraction and to encourage her to stay focused on the new baby that was about to enter our lives. That said, I still felt that unique mixture of emotions only a first-time parent can experience. Overwhelming joy, love, excitement, amazement, exhaustion—and a taste of fear.

Fast forward many years. We now see a role reversal. As I wrote and gave birth to my first book, Kathy was there every step of the way encouraging me to stay focused and being my coach. Her confidence in and support of me throughout this effort has been nothing short of remarkable.

I also want to thank my friend, Kevin Johnson, for his tireless work coaching me throughout the process and for his editing of the manuscript. And to Richard Dodson for all of his work on book cover design and page layout—as well as all of his groundwork leading to actual book publication! Thanks, Kevin and Richard!

It has been an amazing run over the last 40 years. The opportunity to have worked worldwide in six companies—both large and small, public and privately-held—has given me the first-hand insights from which this book was written. In particular, having seen the work up close and personal through my eyes as a senior leader, has provided me with a very clear perspective on what successful senior leaders look like and how they behave. And, of course, what the dysfunctional behaviors of senior leaders also look like!

I want to thank all of the CEOs and senior leaders with whom I have worked and for their genuine courage to lead, not follow. Without these experiences, I would not have been able to capture the essence of this book—the actual stories that bring color and life to the words that are written.

Finally, I would like to deeply thank my family for their unbending support and for their constant love in helping me to be a better parent, husband, father, grandfather, co-worker, neighbor, friend—and now, author. Thanks, Kathy, Brian, Anna, Heather, and Kevin!

About the Author

Thomas Schlick is a transformational leader who has successfully led organizations through high growth as well as difficult turnaround situations. He's held executive roles (COO, EVP, SVP) at some of the world's leading organizations including Johnson & Johnson (Sterilmed) and Emerson.

He earned an MBA from the Carlson School of Management, a Bachelor's Degree in Electrical Engineering from the University of Minnesota, and is a certified Lean Six Sigma Black Belt. He is past President of AFSMI (Association for Service Management International), and currently serves on the advisory boards of The Service Council and the Society for Service Executives.

He particularly enjoys mentoring senior executives through Menttium Corpration, and teaching as an Adjunct Professor at the Hamline University School of Business.

Tom works with corporations and leadership teams experiencing disruptive change. He provides consulting, coaching, and training on both strategy and execution, and speaks at corporate and industry events.

www.JumpstartYourServiceRevolution.com